The Tr

Athol Fugard has been work.   ......atre as a
playwright, director and actor since the mid-fifties in
South Africa, England and the United States. His plays
include: *No-Good Friday, Nongogo, The Blood Knot,
Hello and Goodbye, People Are Living There, Boesman
and Lena, Statements after an Arrest under the
Immorality Act, Sizwe Banzi Is Dead, Dimetos, The
Island, A Lesson from Aloes, 'Master Harold' . . . and
the boys, The Road to Mecca, A Place with the Pigs,
My Children! My Africa!, Playland, Valley Song, The
Captain's Tiger, Sorrows and Rejoicings, Exits and
Entrances, Victory* and *Coming Home*. His work has
been seen on stage in South Africa, London, Broadway,
off-Broadway and in regional theatre in the US. Film
credits include *The Road to Mecca, Gandhi, The Killing
Fields, Meetings with Remarkable Men, Marigolds in
August, Boesman and Lena* and *The Guest*. He has
written the novel *Tsotsi*, a film version of which was
made in South Africa and recently won the Academy
Award for Best Foreign Film, as well as the Michael
Powell Award and the Standard Life Audience Award at
the 2005 Edinburgh Film Festival, the People's Choice
Award at the Toronto Film Festival and the Audience
Award at the Los Angeles AFI Film Festival. He has also
published his autobiographical memoirs, *Cousins*.

from Faber
by the same author

PLAYS ONE
(*The Road to Mecca, A Place with the Pigs,
My Children! My Africa!, Playland, Valley Song*)

ATHOL FUGARD

The Train Driver

faber and faber

First published by the Fugard Theatre, Cape Town,
in association with Junkets Publisher in 2010

First published in Great Britain in 2010
by Faber and Faber Limited
74–77 Great Russell Street, London WC1B 3DA

Typeset by Country Setting, Kingsdown, Kent CT14 8ES
Printed and bound by CPI Group (UK) Ltd, Croydon, CR0 4YY

A CIP record for this book
is available from the British Library

ISBN 978-0-571-27520-5

MIX
Paper from
responsible sources
FSC® C013604

4 6 8 10 9 7 5

For Pumla Lolwana and her three children,
Lindani, Andile and Sesanda, who died on the
railway tracks between Philippi and Nyanga
on the Cape Flats on Friday 8 December 2000

Contents

Pages from a Diary

I

11TH JUNE 2002   I woke up this morning on the coast of Southern California to an overcast grey day and my seventieth birthday. I feel good about it. It comes after a lunatic year in which I directed five productions of my play *Sorrows and Rejoicings* on three continents – an exercise that lived up to the title. It left me physically and emotionally drained and made it easy for me at the end of it to decide that my days as a director were over in much the same way that I decided a few years ago I would not do any more acting. I have no doubts about those decisions. Both roles were forced on me in my early years of making theatre in South Africa when I discovered that no one wanted to touch the plays that I wanted to write. I had no choice but to get up there and have a go at it myself. What surprises me is that I stayed up there for so long because I don't think I have the right temperament for either acting or directing.

I've made a few other resolutions and, taken together, they have given me a sense of adventure as I face up to whatever time is left to me without any clutter to my essential identity as a writer. I've replaced my rickety old table with a beautiful, solid slab of mahogany on four legs – my new 'home', the safest place in my universe because when I sit here I know with something approaching conviction who and what I am.

That year of rehearsal rooms and nerve-wrecking and depressing openings – I never learnt how to cope with them! – gave me no chance to write. All I could do in the succession of hotel rooms was to make a few vacuous entries in this notebook and yearn for the time when

I would be free once again to explore that ultimate *terra incognito*, that most outer of all outer spaces – the blank page.

So here it is, the moment I anticipated so longingly during that muscle-cramping year, and the question is: what now? It's not an intimidating question. I don't think there has ever been a time when I didn't have at least half-a-dozen stories that I knew I had to tell sooner or later. I could page back through this notebook and find many entries short-listing the 'appointments I have to keep'. The trouble is, without exception it has never been left to me to decide when that should be. Nothing would make me happier than to make this the moment I settle down to telling the story of a hot summer's afternoon I spent with my dead and dear friend Barney Simon in the garden of The Ashram – my Port Elizabeth home – watching birds and talking about our lives and work. It would be a celebration of one of the abiding passions of my life – bird-watching – and of one of my most important friendships. But it's the story of Pumla Lolwana that is commanding my attention this morning. It is just over a year and a half since I read about her and her three children for the first time and immediately recognised it as one of those stories I would have an appointment with some day. This is what I read:

---

12 December 2000

MOTHER, THREE CHILDREN DIE IN TRACK SUICIDE

Own Correspondent, Cape Town, Tuesday

A MOTHER with a child on her back and two toddlers in her arms stood on the tracks in front of an oncoming train – and when the five-year-old child tried to scurry away, she pulled him back before the family was pulverised under the train's wheels, *Die Burger* newspaper reported.

The seriously traumatised train driver looked on helplessly as Pumla Lolwana (35), from the Samora Machel squatter camp, and her three children, Lindani (2), Andile (3) and Sesanda (5), died on the railway line between Philippi and Nyanga on the Cape Flats on Friday afternoon.

By Monday night nobody had claimed the bodies of the mother and her three children from the Salt River mortuary. The reason for her suicide, barely two weeks before Christmas, still remains a mystery.

Metro Rail confirmed to *Die Burger* that Lolwana apparently committed suicide. 'The train driver is receiving counselling. He is extremely traumatised, because he saw the drama play out in front of him and wasn't able to stop the train in time,' Metro Rail representative Daphne Kayster said.

An industrial social worker who works with train drivers told *Die Burger* that many people use suicide in front of oncoming suburban trains as their 'way out' when personal problems get too much.

Statistics published at the beginning of this month indicate that approximately 400 people die on the train tracks between Cape Town and Khayelitsha every year.

According to an eyewitness, one of the children managed to escape from his mother's arms. However, she pulled him back and held tightly on to him while the train sped closer. She made no attempt to get away or save her children.

Jaqueline van Rensburg, industrial social worker, who treats up to 15 train drivers a month after accidents, told *Die Burger* that the drivers work under extremely difficult circumstances and feel guilty whenever anybody dies under their train.

'The drivers feel very guilty because they have absolutely no control over the train. A train needs up to 300m to come to a stop. They can't swerve. They very much want to prevent the accident, but they are powerless.'

'Some of the train drivers whom I have spoken to say they always wonder about the victims' families and put themselves in that person's shoes. In the long term these incidents have a negative impact on train drivers.'

I read the story in the internet edition of the *Mail and Guardian*. I have now copied it out, word for word, by hand, into this notebook. I did that because I feel the need to possess it at a very personal level, to make it a part of my life. I ask myself, yet again: this moment of 'recognition' that has been such a recurring experience in my writing life – what is it all about? How does it work? Why is it that certain stories, faces or incidents in the thousands that crowd my daily life will separate themselves from the others and take on an imperative quality that demands I deal with them, which for me means writing about them.

In 1988, at a time when reports of the latest horrors of Apartheid were crowding each other on the front pages of our local Port Elizabeth newspaper, it was a little three-inch item hidden away on the back pages that really stopped me. The headline story was about the massacre of twenty people when the police opened fire on a funeral procession of a political activist. I was horrified, but I moved on until I came to the story of Anela Myalatya, a schoolteacher in a small country town who had been necklaced by an angry mob because the word had gone around that he was an informer. After reading it again and then again, I fetched a pair of scissors, cut it out and pasted it into my notebook.

Is it as simple as Stalin's cynical remark that a thousand deaths are a statistic and one death a tragedy? That is what a writer is always looking for – a strong story with an unhappy ending. In my case, however, I know that there is something else at work, something less easy to define. It involves one of my more important instincts as a writer because *it* has chosen the stories I decide to tell. What I recognised in that image, face, incident or three-inch newspaper story was the possibility of looking at something in myself, even though in most cases I was not aware of this at the time. Only afterwards did I realise that they were a shield I had held up so that I could slay a private Medusa.

That was certainly so with Anela Myalatya. *My Children! My Africa!*, the play I based on that three-inch item in the newspaper, is a very political statement about a moment in my country's history, but it is also an intensely personal one. I have correctly described Mr M – the schoolteacher in my play – as an attempt at self-portraiture. His passions for learning and language, his belief in evolution rather than violent revolution . . . all of those faiths and qualities, as well as his serious flaws, are mine. I was not consciously aware of any of this when I started writing the play. In fact, if I had had that deliberate intention I doubt very much if that play or any of the others would have been written. Those 'intentions' are secrets that must be kept from even the writer himself.

So this morning it is Pumla Lolwana's story that I will try to live with. Somewhere in his writing Rilke advises a young poet to strive for a degree of innocence when he confronts blank paper and the start of a new adventure. I am not young and innocence is hard to come by now – so many words on paper lie behind this moment! – but I know it is good advice and I will try as hard as I can to follow it. In this instance I am certainly innocent of intentions or expectations. I don't know what will come, if anything, out of that newspaper story.

2

13TH JUNE My usual sunset walk along the beach in the late afternoon, and for a change the sky was clear; at this time of the year the sun generally sets behind a bank of fog waiting far out on the horizon to come drifting in during the night. After a few days of strong spring tides and heavy surf the sea was again very calm with hardly enough energy to uncurl a few small waves close inshore. In the two years I've been here, I've never seen a really wild sea like the ones I grew up with in the Eastern Cape of South Africa when South Atlantic gales lashed the coast. Halfway along my walk I did something that doesn't come easily to me in America: I switched off my neurotic obsession with time. I sat down on the sand with no other intention than to watch the setting sun. Here on the beach, as so many times in the Karoo, it was a gentle breeze – this one off the sea playing on my skin – that turned the mystery of time and its passing into a physical experience. The sunset was simple and serene – a huge smoky orange globe trailing a wake of golden light as it dropped slowly to the horizon. I began to think about Pumla Lolwana again.

The morning session at my table had started with another close reading of the newspaper story. I took up each sentence and looked at it as carefully as I do the beautiful wave-polished pebbles I pick up on my beach walks. I held each sentence for a few seconds, turning it over and over so as to examine it still more carefully before putting it back in its place on the page and moving on. The sentence I couldn't let go of easily, that I kept going back to and looking at again and again, was the opening one.

> A MOTHER with a child on her back and two toddlers in her arms stood on the tracks in front of an oncoming train – and when the five-year-old child tried to scurry away, she pulled him back before the family was pulverised under the train's wheels.

My mind stumbled and fell over itself in trying to deal with that sentence. I couldn't take it in, truly understand it in a way that made it possible for me to move on. Was it because I couldn't 'see' it? The sentence is profoundly disturbing, it has a fierce energy, but when I tried to turn it into a picture my mind refused to move, all it could do was stare at the horror of it. Because the idea alone – a mother commits suicide and kills her three children with herself – is not enough for me as a writer. Ideas never have been. Some sort of picture or image has been the starting point to everything I have written and I need one now, but try as I may I can't break the paralysing effect of that sentence. Pumla Lolwana is shrouded in a darkness my imagination can't penetrate. I've tried to unblock it by imagining the sound of those few dreadful seconds – the children's cries, specially the little boy struggling to get away because he knew what his mother was trying to do, and their names, their beautiful names! Surely she called them out when she tried to comfort and calm them as the train got closer, and then the noise of the train itself, the hooter, the screech of brakes – but even that ploy didn't work. I went through the story again hoping I might have overlooked something that would set me off, but it was a pointless exercise; I already knew the story by heart and I knew there wasn't anything that would help me to build a picture of her. With a growing sense of frustration I put her aside and turned to other work.

Sitting there on the beach at the end of the day, watching the sky fade through a spectrum of soft pastel colours, I had to ask myself why my imagination wasn't working for me this time. Why wasn't it taking control of the facts as laid out and creating a plausible fiction as it had done so many times in the past fifty years of writing? I'd never known it to hesitate in that way before. Why now? Was it that it felt it didn't have the right – that much vaunted writer's liberty and licence – to do that this time? Why not just go back to my table tonight and, in exactly the same way as I put the schoolteacher of the three-inch newspaper story into a tired old double-breasted suit in my imagination, see the young mother standing there on the tracks waiting for the train *barefoot*? That one detail might be the trigger I was looking for.

That little surge of hope didn't last long. I had a growing sense that this time I was without any rights to liberty or licence. Apart from the fact that suicide is something I know I will never understand, will always be a mystery to me, there is something about the story of Pumla Lolwana and her three children that would make feeding it to my writer's ego obscene. As for just witnessing it . . . I can't even do that because I don't in fact know if she was wearing shoes or if she and the children were barefoot.

3

14TH JUNE   As an alternative to the beach I sometimes walk next to the railway line that connects San Diego to Los Angeles. The regular traffic on this line is the blue and white Coaster, a local suburban commuter train with a blaring organ-like note for a hooter, and less frequently the blue and silver Surfliner, which goes with only a few stops all the way to Los Angeles. A few times during the day and night long freight trains also travel along this line. I saw a real beauty yesterday – forty-five coaches and wagons long and all of them with the name 'Barnum and Bailey Circus' proudly emblazoned on their sides.

The walk is a lovely but mildly illegal one. There are signs in Spanish and English warning there is danger and that I am trespassing on railway property, but none of the joggers and walkers who use the path pay any attention to them. Along this stretch of the line the tracks are only a few yards in from the edge of a cliff – there is just enough room for the footpath and a swathe of purple statice and clumps of elegant pampas grass. Standing at the edge of the cliff you have the delight of gulls and pelicans floating by at chest level. A few hundred feet below a mostly blue and smiling Pacific Ocean rolls on to a clean white beach, its only debris those beautiful stones I pick up and discard, and clumps of kelp. Dolphins play in these waters and at the right time of the year whales can be spotted on their way to and from their mating grounds off the coast of Mexico. There is one other very southern Californian detail in this scene: the little black figures on their long boards, waiting for the perfect wave along the line where the surf first heaves up to come rolling in.*

The passengers on the trains headed north to Oceanside, San Clemente, San Juan Capistrano, Irvine, Santa Ana, Anaheim, Fullerton and Los Angeles – all of them neat Spanish-style stations with attractive floral features – enjoy wonderful views of the sea and coastline. It is a very different experience to that of the commuters travelling from Khayelitsha, through Nonkqubela, Nolungile, Mandalay, Philippi, Nyanga, Heideveld, Netreg, Bonte-heuwel, Langa, Mutual, Ysterplaat, Paarden Eiland, to Cape Town. A friend sent me a copy of a video which is shown to train drivers on this route as part of their six-month training programme. It takes you from the driver's point of view on the fifty-minute ride through a landscape of soul-crushing squalor. At the best of times the sandy, wind-blown Cape Flats have little or no appeal. The ulcerous squatter camps of miserable shanties and *pondoks* which line this route into the mother city are dumping grounds of hopeless human lives. Our proud slogan 'The

* Life on the side of the tracks – Southern California – the world of the bronzed body beautiful – stay fit, stay beautiful – joggers, mountain bikes, walkers with dogs, couples with prams, surfers slipping down the crevices in the cliff face . . .

Cape of Good Hope' a cruel misnomer for the world these people live in.

Thirty years ago, in my play *Boesman and Lena* I made a drunk and embittered Boesman describe their *pondok* on the mudflats of the Swartkops River as 'white man's rubbish'. In a paroxysm of self-hatred he goes on to say: 'We pick it up, we wear it, we eat it, we're made of it now . . . we're white man's rubbish.' That was the old Apartheid South Africa. This is the brave new South Africa. The people who live in those *pondoks* on the Cape Flats – structures every bit as flimsy and useless against the elements as the one Boesman built – can't single out the white man as the source of their rubbish any more, but in essence the refrain is the same: they live in a world made out of rubbish, they are the rubbish of that world.

Boesman and Lena was my first deep journey into the world of the *pondok*, a world that had fascinated me from childhood when I used to accompany my mom to a butcher in a humble little Coloured settlement on the outskirts of Port Elizabeth to buy black-market meat for our boarding house during the strictly rationed years of the Second World War. The nearest I can get to explaining that fascination – it is even here in Southern California when I see the simple homes of Mexican labourers – is to point to the elemental power and resonance that the gestures and things in those lives acquire because they are so poverty stricken, so reduced to essentials. All my life it has been those humble and desperate little worlds that have fired my imagination; I have studied them and tried to imagine my way into their secret life as eagerly and passionately as others do with the palaces and mansions of the mighty. When Lena breaks and shares her crust of brown bread with Outa, as they sit huddled together in the cold of the Swartkops mudflats, it is the profound simplicity of those elements that turn that moment into a mass, a bitter celebration of her life. That crust of brown bread and mug of bitter and black tea become sacramental: 'Bitter and Black' she says. 'The bread should have bruises . . . it's my life, Outa.' A loaf of fresh white bread in the hands of a comfortable suburban housewife could never resonate in that way.

In writing *Boesman and Lena* I put together all the clues I had accumulated over the years in trying to find my way into the heart of that reality. I believe I succeeded.
I revisited that play recently with a student production at the University of California in San Diego and I can say now with conviction that there are no falsehoods in it. So having made that imaginative journey on the mudflats should it not now be possible for me, in a similar fashion, to crawl into the *pondok* in the Samora Machel informal settlement where Pumla Lolwana and her three children lived?

The story of South African poverty, like the story of poverty anywhere, is made up of a few very stark elements, starting with hunger and ending, as must have been the case with Pumla Lolwana, with a loss of hope. Within that terrible little span of human experience there are a few variables that can be assembled in different patterns. In her case those variables most likely included the loss of the breadwinner, her man, the father of her children. It could have been a death – those 'informal settlements' are violent worlds – it could have been desertion, a man looking for his 'way out' when the burden of a wife and three children became too much. Given those possibilities can't I just get on with it, for God's sake, and give Pumla Lolwana a fictional reality and deal with her in the way that I did with Boesman and Lena? I wish I could, but the answer is again 'no'. Boesman and Lena wanted to live. As devastating as that night on the mudflats had been for both of them, they are on their feet at the end, they walk away from that cold campfire and the dead black man even though it is a walk into darkness. Implicit in that walk is their will to live – an unconscious act of faith in the next day's sunrise. That is the fundamental act of faith in my life: there will be a tomorrow worth living.

That is why I shied away from an earlier challenge to confront final despair. The real Helen Martins of my play *The Road to Mecca* died in agony, caustic soda eating away her insides because she had lost faith in herself. That is not how my telling of her extraordinary story ends. I used my 'liberty and licence' as a storyteller to create a note of affirmation after she confronts the extinction of her creativity. I can't play any fictional games with Pumla Lolwana. That moment when she stands on the railway lines, fiercely holding on to her children, too final.

4

17TH JUNE   I was back next to the tracks this afternoon. I took a moment when I was sure there were no trains coming to stand between them and stare along their length. I had never given them a second thought before reading Pumla Lolwana's story; now, those two parallel rails of steel fascinate me. There was something hypnotic and strangely menacing in the illusion of convergence as they stretched away from me. The same thing has happened to the trains that come charging past on my walks. They are huge double-decker leviathans with the driver's cab at the top level. Up until now I've enjoyed them innocently as images of energy and splendour, which is how the old steam engines of my youth used to thrill me in Port Elizabeth. Now they also have become unnerving, their power and momentum, their unstoppable force very frightening. The adrenaline rush that comes as they thunder past is no longer the elating thrill of my boyhood: it is fear.

One of them, a northbound Coaster, passed me on this afternoon's walk. I heard it before I saw it – a raucous blare from its horn as it left the Penasquitos Marsh and came rushing out from under the road bridge. Although I couldn't see the driver I gave him a wave as the train passed. I don't suppose he even noticed me.

The Cape Town commuter trains are single-deckers, so those drivers do not ride as high and mighty as their American cousins. By comparison, the driver of the train that killed Pumla Lolwana and her children would have had a very intimate relationship with her as she stood there waiting. His was most probably the last human face she saw, provided she kept her eyes open until the end. It is a thought that stops time: the two of them looking at each other, seeing each other, locked into a moment that will end the life of the mother and her children and scar his for ever. The rest of my walk is a blank. The thought of those few seconds between the woman and the train driver haunted me all the way back to this table. I returned to the newspaper report and read:

> 'The train driver is receiving counselling. He is extremely traumatised, because he saw the drama play out in front of him and wasn't able to stop the train in time.'

It takes three hundred metres for one of these trains travelling at a speed of seventy kph to stop. But he most probably didn't. The instructions to the driver in the event of an accident on this line are very specific:

> *If the driver is between stations he must not stop. The body will be behind him and he must continue to the next station. There he must report the incident via radio, and have the police and rescue services called.*

I've never really given the driver much thought, but now it occurs to me that he could possibly help me see her. If I could live through a night on the Swartkops mudflats with Boesman and Lena, then couldn't I sit in the cab with the train driver for that fatal afternoon run from Khayelitsha to Cape Town? Unlike the mother, so emphatically identified by her name, 'Pumla Lolwana', and those of her children, his very anonymity is a help. It is in fact hugely liberating. For the first time since starting to live with that newspaper story I feel a surge of energy and excitement because I realise I am free to create a fictional identity.

So here goes. His name will be 'Roelf Visagie', a strong, no-nonsense, down-to-earth Afrikaans name. The railways in South Africa have always been the preserve of the Afrikaner, and if there is one South African identity I empathise with it is them – my mother's people. I know I've chosen a good name because without any effort on my side 'Roelf Visagie' has attracted to itself images from the life of a friend of mine in Port Elizabeth, a fishing companion of many years.

The training video that was sent me from Cape Town included interviews with and images of the drivers at the controls of the train. Their faces were those of decent but deeply troubled men who had not been able to stop in time – they had all had their 'hits', the word used by one of them to describe those accidents. They spoke in muted tones about what it meant because 'It's a life you're taking, another human being . . . and you never forget the first one – no matter how many hits you have after that, you never forget the first one. Doesn't matter what it is – a cow, or a dog or an old man – its all the same, it's a life you've taken.'

My Roelf Visagie would be at home in their company, drinking a cold Castle or a brandy and Coke and talking about the general fuck-up of the world. For all his rough edges, my fishing friend in Port Elizabeth was also a good man; he had the same reverence for life that I saw in the faces and heard in the voices of the men in the video.

So I decided it was going to be my Roelf Visagie's first hit – that is the dangerous side of writing, playing God with the fictional lives you've created. He of course had no idea what I had in store for him that Friday afternoon. If anything his life felt and looked particularly good as he settled down in the driver's cab for the run to Cape Town. He had a devoted wife and two lovely children – a boy and a girl – a nice house in a quiet suburb and, to complete the picture, he was a white man with a job, and a reasonably well-paid one at that with a pension fund and medical scheme – no mean achievement in the new South Africa.

But what really gave his spirits a lift when he got the signal to pull out of Khayelitsha station that afternoon were his fishing prospects for the coming weekend. He was going to join two buddies for a trip up the West Coast to look for steenbras. They were going to make a whole weekend of it, sleeping on the beach and returning for work early on Monday. When the train pulled into Nonkqubela station, Roelfie was imagining the campfire, the lovely barbecue smell of chops and *boerewors* sizzling away on the coals; at Nolungile it was that electrifying moment when a fishing-reel ratchet suddenly starts screaming in the middle of the night and, still half asleep, you scramble for your rod because you know a steenbras has picked you up. The next stations were Mandalay and Philippi and once again the train pulled in and pulled out on time and Roelf Visagie, with his hands on the brake and accelerator, luxuriated in the sense that his life, like his train, was under control.

The training video gives a good picture of what the drivers on this Khayelitsha–Cape Town route have to contend with. There are fences on each side of the track which are meant to keep people off, but these have been broken down or torn through in places so as to provide a short cut between the squatter camps on either side. In the video one constantly sees people walking next to the tracks or making suicidal dashes across them in front of the oncoming train.

With all that going on Roelf Visagie would hardly have noticed the woman way ahead, quietly waiting. But even if he had seen her – a mother with a baby on her back and two children in her arms – what of it? He must have seen at least half a dozen like her already on this run. In any case – come now, man! – a mother and her children? She's not about to go and do something stupid . . . until suddenly there she is in front of him with one of the children struggling to break loose, looking up at him, and Roelf Visagie starts to live through a few seconds that will haunt him for the rest of his life. He has his hand on the brake, his foot on the hooter, he is shouting and swearing, but it makes no difference. His life is out of control. It is over in a flash.

It wouldn't have been long before a crowd gathered, pressed against the fence or crawling through its holes for a closer look at the remains of Pumla Lolwana and her three children. And angry! Oh yes, very angry. Very loud angry voices.

'*Haai liewe here*. Look at them! How many is it? A mother and three children for God's sake. Is there no bloody justice in the world? Didn't that bloody driver see her? Why didn't that fucking white man stop?'

That is why head office has ordered the drivers to carry on to the next station in the event of an accident.

5

20TH JUNE   Another alternative to my beach walk is along a stretch of 'Historic Highway 101' as it skirts the Penasquitos Marsh. This one gives me a chance to study the wonderful variety of water birds. It is also a schizoid experience, as it involves walking the line between two starkly contrasting worlds: stretching away from me on one side is the serene marsh, its self-contained silence broken only by the high, piping calls of curlews and sandpipers and, on the other, just a few feet away from me as I walk along the very narrow verge, the never-ending rush and roar of traffic on the Highway. This evening, the birds were all there in the distance waiting in the muddy channels for the incoming tide to reach them: herons and egrets, long-billed curlews and whimbrels and godwits, sandpipers and plovers. I had my binoculars focused on a great blue heron when a blue and white Coaster train rode into its field of vision. Distance and the soft light of the evening had once again made it very innocent, a thing of beauty; it could so easily have been a little toy train on the floor of a young boy's bedroom and not the terrible instrument a despairing soul would use to end a life.

Back at my table I read:

> 'The train driver is receiving counselling. He is extremely traumatised, because he saw the drama play out in front of him and wasn't able to stop the train in time.'

And then at the end of the story:

> Jaqueline van Rensburg, industrial social worker, who treats up to fifteen train drivers a month after accidents, told *Die Burger* that the drivers work under extremely difficult circumstances and feel guilty whenever anybody dies under their train.
>
> 'The drivers feel very guilty because they have absolutely no control over the train.'

In the training video the drivers talk about the trauma. The advice given to them by the social worker is to talk about it – the sooner the better and to anyone who will listen.

That is the advice a sympathetic Miss Jacqueline van Rensburg gives a hesitant Mr Visagie when he sits down awkwardly in her office. The likes of Roelfie Visagie do not take easily to counselling, and even less so when it comes from a woman, but Miss van Rensburg knows this – he is not the first driver to come to her for help.

> Whatever you are feeling don't keep it bottled up inside you, Mr Visagie. Talking will help you take control of the experience and put it behind you so that you can get on with your life.

But Mr Visagie does not find it easy. It takes a lot of patience and gentle nudging before the words start to come, very haltingly at first as he clumsily feels his way into the emotional chaos inside him. She listens and watches carefully as he talks, reading signs of anger and confusion, pain and guilt.

> *Ja*, I know, Miss. I know it's not really my fault, everybody keeps telling me that, you, my wife, the other drivers – some of them have already had as many as twenty hits! – *ja*, that's what they call it, a hit. 'It's because it's your first one, Visagie,' they say to me. 'That's why it's so hard. But give it time. You'll get over it.' I get so the hell in when people tell me that, Miss. *Ja*. You as well. I know you are all just trying to help me so I don't mean to be offensive but I mean what the hell, if it's not my fault – and I don't need anybody to tell me that any more! – then whose fault is it? *Ja*, why doesn't somebody try telling me that for a change instead of all this . . .

He leaves the sentence unfinished. Miss van Rensburg interprets the restless movement of his hands as the need for a cigarette. She tells him he can smoke if he wants to. He shakes his head.

Must we point our fingers at Metrorail? *Ja*, why not? They don't fix up the fences on the side of the tracks where the people have broken them down? God didn't just put her down there on those tracks, you know. She and her children crawled through one of those holes to get there. I've given up reporting them any more because nobody listens. Or maybe it's the Government to blame. Maybe they should take some time off from driving around in their big Mercedes Benzes and give those people decent houses to live in. You take off some time one day, Miss, and go and look at those *pondoks*. My dog's kennel in our backyard is better than what those people is living in. And then of course there's the woman herself. Because don't think I've forgotten her. I wish I could. But even if I could my wife wouldn't let me because that's who she points the finger at. *Ja*, good old Lynette.

'She's the one who did it, Roelfie darling. Nobody dragged her and her children on to the railway lines. I don't know how a mother could do a thing like that but she did. I bet you anything you like she was drunk. So you see, *liefling*, it's not your fault.'

Just like that. I got it from her again this morning. I had another bad night you see. I took the pills the doctor gave me, but the trouble is sort of . . . *Ag*, what the hell . . . I'm sort of frightened of going to sleep because even with the pills if I wake up it starts again, over and over – I'm looking at the tracks and then . . . I swear to God I didn't see her until suddenly there she is in front of me, waiting for me, with the children. Anyway, that is how my day started – with Lynette walking around the room, getting ready to go to her job at 'Pick and Pay' and I can see she's the hell-in because she also didn't get much sleep because of me, but she is trying so hard to hide it while she tells Roelfie darling that it isn't his fault and how could a mother do a thing like that and please, *liefling*, go and see you doctor again and ask him for bigger pills because these little ones isn't knocking you out . . .

And while I'm sitting there on the bed watching her and listening I'm also seeing pictures of that world on the side of the tracks and it makes me *naar*, you know, like I want to vomit because it's all there inside me now, *ja*, that for my Christmas bonus this year I got a whole rotten stinking bloody squatter camp inside me, choking me so badly I can't tell Lynette to shut the fuck up because she doesn't know what she is talking about, she doesn't know anything. But even if she did, even if she did turn off the hair-dryer and give me a chance for a change, what would I say to her? What can I say to you, Miss, who finds it so easy to tell me it wasn't my fault because she was 'looking for a way out of her troubles'? Do you know about those 'personal problems'? If I ever get back to driving you must take a ride with me one day – Khayelitsha to Cape Town. I'll point out the beauty spots. We'll do it in winter when a good Cape storm has left that whole world under six inches of water. Then you will see then, in the early morning, the mothers with their babies in their arms standing outside their *pondoks* because there was no place to lie down inside. That's when you start to ask questions, Miss. How long have they been standing? All night? How they going to cook food for the children?

Pause. This time he lights a cigarette. Ms van Rensburg revises a mental note she was going to put into his file: it's not anger she's watching, it's rage.

So you see, Miss, why she did it is not the problem. *Ag* no, who wants to live like that? Who wants tomorrow if it means your children are going to be living like that? And while they're living getting murdered, or raped or ending up with AIDS and everything else. No, to hell with it. I understand why she did it. Any sensible mother would drag her kids through a hole in the fence on to those tracks if that is all they could hope for. No, Miss, my problem is why the hell did she have to go and choose my train? Why didn't she wait for the guy with his twenty hits? He knows how to forget her. Instead she chooses me. No, don't shake your head! She was standing there waiting for me and I couldn't say, 'No thank you, lady, not today.' That's what people like you don't understand. There was no way out for me, Miss. I couldn't swerve, I couldn't stop the fucking train. *Ja*, there's another joke for you if you want one. 'The controls!' 'The train driver must remain in control of the train at all times.' Bullshit! I had no more control over the train when she stood there then I did over the day I was born. If you really want to know something, Miss, I'm not so sure any more I got control over anything. And let me tell you something else: I'm not the only one. *Ja*. You too! Sitting there behind your desk and looking like you're 'in control'! That driver's cab is a trap, Miss, and we're all in there one way or another. We can see it coming, we're heading towards it at ninety kilometres an hour, but we can't swerve and the instructions from head office is 'Don't stop, just leave the bloody mess behind you and carry on.'

And that is as far as I go with Roelf Visagie. I could follow him out of that counselling session into the rest of his life, the passing of time that will turn his raw wound into a scar, sit one night around a campfire on the beach with Des and Dennis waiting for a ratchet to scream – but in doing that I would also be leaving behind the mess of the tracks between Philippi and Nyanga and I can't do that.*

6

24TH JUNE   For a change I was in a train, a Surfliner headed north to Los Angeles. I was on my way to watch an understudy rehearsal and to say goodbye to the wonderful cast of *Sorrows and Rejoicings*, which was in the last week of its run in LA. I settled back in my comfortable business-class seat, determined for once to do nothing other than look out of the window and enjoy the long stretch of beautiful scenery. But old habits don't break easily so I kept my notebook and pen in my lap. And just as well. Darwin called it his *cacoethes scribendi*, his incurable itch to write. I suffer from the same complaint. It wasn't long before I had forgotten about the scenery and was scribbling away.

---

* But I don't know that anything is any clearer. Pumla Lolwana still stands inviolate on the tracks between Philippi and Nyanga. Instead of being in the cab with him, I feel more like one of the passengers in the coaches behind – wondering why the train is taking so long to pull away from Nyanga station and seeing officials running about on the platform outside and then hearing talk about a woman and three children . . .

It had started with a delay at Oceanside station because of work on the track. It made me wonder if there had been a parallel experience for the passengers in the coaches behind Roelf Visagie? Had they started looking out of the window as I had just done, wondering what had gone wrong and how long the delay would be? Then seeing officials running around outside on the platform and hearing talk about a woman and three children. It was a sobering and depressing thought. It suggested that maybe that was all I could ever hope to be – a passenger in the train that had killed a mother and her children, getting scraps of second-hand news about their deaths and impatient for the train to move on.

My return journey to San Diego was late at night and my notebook was again in my lap – the itch to scratch away at a blank page now even stronger than in the morning. The cab ride from the station to the theatre had passed the County Courthouse, which had immediately brought LaShanda Crozier back into my life. Her story was carried by the *Los Angeles Times* ten days after I had read about Pumla Lolwana. It was then just three days before Christmas. Her story is also a file on my computer.

Friday 22 December 2000

TROUBLED LIFE LED TO THREE DEATHS

TRAGEDY: Many people saw LaShanda Crozier's personal and financial problems, but no sign that she would throw her two daughters off a courthouse ledge, then jump.

When LaShanda Crozier pushed her two daughters to their deaths off the downtown County Courthouse and followed them down, it ended a spell of economic and personal hardship, neighbors, relatives and authorities said Thursday. Crozier, 27, had talked of suffering a miscarriage that cost her a job, seeing her boyfriend lose a job, and facing eviction – the threat that brought her to the courthouse, they said.

Hours after reaching an out-of-court agreement with her landlord to gradually pay $925 in back rent, Crozier pushed daughters Breanna, 7, and Joan, 5, from the ninth-floor ledge and then jumped herself.

Her boyfriend, the girls' father, left the courthouse after the hearing and did not witness the deaths, authorities said. He said Thursday, 'I have not come to terms with what happened to my children.' He also said he was angry at Crozier, whom he described as selfish. 'She should have called me at work.'

Crozier owed back rent on the $400-a-month apartment unit near Exposition Park that she shared with the girls and their father.

In a hallway outside Courtroom 547 on Wednesday, as they waited for the judge, Crozier and landlord Raul Almendariz tried to negotiate an agreement. He offered to allow the family to stay in their cramped, ground-floor quarters if they would start paying weekly installments of about $150. As an alternative, Almendariz offered to let Crozier out of the lease – and the back payments – if she would move the family out right after Jan. 1.

Almendariz said Crozier wanted to stay, even though a recent rough patch had left the couple with little money.

He said the couple told him that Crozier had spent a few days in a hospital after losing a child to a miscarriage, and that the episode cost her a job cleaning rooms at a local hotel. The boyfriend said that he had lost one of his two jobs because of the Metropolitan Transportation Authority bus drivers' strike and that his other job paid just $250 a week.

'She seemed embarrassed yesterday, about the whole situation,' Almendariz said. 'She didn't try to make any excuses at all. She said she would just like the opportunity to stay in the apartment and catch up on the rent.'

Almendariz said he agreed. Crozier signed the court papers and headed outside and into the sunshine with her boyfriend and children in tow.

Stunned family members on Thursday described Crozier as a troubled woman who had struggled economically, emotionally and in a stormy relationship with her boyfriend. They said that in recent years she had occasionally given up custody of the two girls to an aunt, Marietta Snowden.

'She was sometimes unstable,' said Snowden. 'My niece was withdrawn.'

Snowden also said she had been trying to retain custody of the two girls, citing her concerns about Crozier's relationship with her boyfriend, the poor living conditions at the apartment complex and Crozier's mental state. But 'nobody listened, nobody listened, nobody listened,' she said.

Snowden described Breanna as an outgoing tomboy who was fiercely protective of her little sister. Joan, she said, was shy and quiet, a 'pretty little girl who loved to wear high-heeled sneakers.'

Snowden said Breanna sensed there was something wrong with her mother and father. 'She said, "Auntie, I love my mama, but I don't want to stay with her."'

Almendariz, like so many others who had crossed paths with Crozier, said that in recent days she had shown no signs of irrational behavior or flashes of anger or depression. There was nothing to signal that she was capable of pushing the two girls off a ledge and then jumping herself.

Witnesses later told police the two objects they saw Crozier push or throw over the ledge were the two girls.

Both landed on a fourth-floor ledge and were taken to County-USC Medical Center, where they died a short time later.

Crozier landed on the ground and was pronounced dead at the scene. Los Angeles police continued to investigate the matter Thursday, and court officials reviewed their files to glean hints to what might have prompted Crozier's actions.

Crozier was described by neighbors as friendly but quiet and somewhat guarded.

She and her boyfriend kept to themselves. And they argued occasionally behind closed doors, the neighbors said.

'They had their problems,' said Zelaya, but no more than anyone else in the run-down building a block west of the Los Angeles Coliseum and the USC campus.

LAPD Capt. Charlie Beck said the boyfriend was trying in vain Thursday to come to terms with what had happened.

'He's doing awful,' Beck said. 'How do you even begin to understand the kind of pain that this is causing somebody?

'We will be talking to him again, see if he can put some shred of reason to this,' said Beck. 'But he didn't have anything he could offer . . . I don't think there is an answer for this that anyone but she will ever know.'

Penelope Trickett, a developmental psychologist and professor of social work at USC, acknowledged the perplexing nature of cases in which suicidal parents choose to kill their children.

'I think it has something to do with a bond between parents and kids,' she said. 'The feeling you are one entity, you and your children, and that if there is no hope for you, there is no hope for the children.'

Landlord Almendariz said he was haunted Thursday by his last image of Crozier.

As they left the courthouse, he had just given her older daughter Breanna a $20 bill and told her to share it with her little sister as a Christmas present. The little girl politely said 'Thank you,' and 'Yes, I will,' he said.

He said, Crozier seemed a little sad but nothing more.

'I wish I could have talked to her a little bit more. Told her, you know, things are going to be OK, that people have their ups and downs. I wish there was something somebody could have done to help,' he added.

'Somebody should have known how depressed she was.'

Apart from its own unique horror, what struck me about this story as compared with that of Pumla Lolwana was the wealth of personal detail and the expressions of concern and sorrow by neighbours, relatives and authorities. What vivid hints there are, for example, of the characters and Breanna and Joan's relationship and, in contrast, what absence of detail about Andile, Lindani and Sesanda. I did a word count: 1,266 for LaShanda Crozier, 408 for Pumla Lolwana. I have tried to establish if there were any follow-up stories about Pumla Lolwana that might possibly have given some information about her life and circumstances, but I couldn't find any. I have to ask myself: is there any significance in this? Do we South Africans put a lower value on life? Have we been so insensitised, so numbed by our long history of violence, the prevalence of poverty and famine in Africa, the constant bombardment by the media of stories and images of starving mothers and children on this God-forsaken continent that the death of another mother and her three children merits only a bland and relatively impersonal report, which gives more space to the trauma of the train driver than to the victims of the tragedy? I almost regret now that I know their names. It fosters the illusion that I could somehow get to know them, understand something about what happened on that Friday afternoon. Anonymity would have disillusioned me of that and made even more stark the destitution of that tragic family.

At the end of *My Children! My Africa!*, my Mr M, just before he goes out to confront an angry mob in what amounts to an act of self-immolation, bares his soul to the young Thami in a long monologue which ends with this passage:

> I was ten years old and we were on our way to a rugby match at Somerset East. The lorry stopped at the top of the mountain so that we could stretch our legs and relieve ourselves. It was a hard ride on the back of that lorry. The road hadn't been tarred yet. So there I was, ten years old and sighing with relief as I aimed for the little bush. It was a hot day. The sun right over our heads . . . not a cloud in the vast blue sky. I looked out . . . it's very high up there at the top of the pass . . . and there it was, stretching away from the foot of the mountain, the great pan of the Karoo . . . stretching away forever it seemed into the purple haze and heat of the horizon. Something grabbed my heart at that moment, my soul, and squeezed it until there were tears in my eyes. I had never seen anything so big, so beautiful in all my life. I went to the teacher who was with us and asked him: 'Teacher, where will I come to if I start walking that way?' . . . and I pointed. He laughed. 'Little man,' he said, 'that way is north. If you start walking that way and just keep on walking, and your legs don't give in, you will see all of Africa! Yes, Africa, little man! You will see the great rivers of the continent:

the Vaal, the Zambesi, the Limpopo, the Congo and then the mighty Nile. You will see the mountains: the Drakensberg, Kilimanjaro, Kenya and the Ruwenzori. And you will meet all our brothers: the little Pygmies of the forests, the proud Masai, the Watusi . . . tallest of the tall and the Kikuyu standing on one leg like herons in a pond waiting for a frog.' 'Has teacher seen all that?' I asked. 'No,' he said. 'Then how does teacher know it's there?' 'Because it is all in the books and I have read the books and if you work hard in school, little man, you can do the same without worrying about your legs giving in.'

He was right, Thami. I have seen it. It is all there in the books just as he said it was and I have made it mine. I can stand on the banks of all those great rivers, look up at the majesty of all those mountains, whenever I want to. It is a journey I have made many times. Whenever my spirit was low and I sat alone in my room, I said to myself: 'Walk, Anela! Walk!' . . . and I imagined myself at the foot of the Wapadsberg setting off for that horizon that called me that day forty years ago. It always worked! When I left that little room, I walked back into the world a proud man, because I was an African and all the splendour was my birthright.

(*Pause.*) I don't want to make that journey again, Thami. There is someone waiting for me now at the end of it who has made mockery of all my visions of splendour. He has in his arms my real birthright. I saw him on the television in the Reverend Mbopa's lounge. An Ethiopian tribesman, and he was carrying the body of a little child that had died of hunger in the famine . . . a small bundle carelessly wrapped in a few rags. I couldn't tell how old the man was. The lines of despair and starvation on his face made him look as old as Africa itself.

He held that little bundle very lightly as he shuffled along to a mass grave, and when he reached it, he didn't have the strength to kneel and lay it down gently . . . He just opened his arms and let it fall. I was very upset when the programme ended. Nobody had thought to tell us his name and whether he was the child's father, or grandfather, or uncle. And the same for the baby! Didn't it have a name? How dare you show me one of our children being thrown away and not tell me its name! I demand to know who is in that bundle!

(*Pause.*) Not knowing their names doesn't matter any more. They are more than just themselves. The tribesmen and dead child do duty for all of us, Thami. Every African soul is either carrying that bundle or in it.

What is wrong with this world that it wants to waste you all like that . . . my children . . . my Africa!

Standing there on the railway line between Philippi and Nyanga, with her children in her arms, Pumla Lolwana joins that Ethiopian tribesman with a matching and terrifying loneliness; a Stabat Mater Dolorosa without a redeeming Christ on the cross.

7

27TH JUNE   It is either late at night or very early in the morning and I am lying awake in bed. I resist looking at the luminous dial of my wristwatch because I know that it will only make going back to sleep more difficult. But for once I am not fretting about my insomnia, I am listening to a freight train – it is heading south – and I can both hear and feel the vibrations of passing train traffic in my bedroom. This is a long one and I try to count the individual trucks as they trundle heavily over the bridge in the marsh but after a few seconds I loose count because whenever I hear a passing train these days I end up thinking about Pumla Lolwana. How close was her *pondok* to the railway line? Did she lie awake at night listening to passing trains? Is that how she got the idea? Playing back the images I have of her final moments, there is one which surprisingly and for reasons that elude me, I seem to have a dark sympathy with, almost an understanding: it is the moment when Sesanda tried to escape and she pulled him back and held on to him fiercely as the train sped closer.

'If you live, so must I, but I can't, I can't . . .'

And that last walk of hers with the children. It would have been dramatic to picture it in pouring rain, mother and children drenched to the skin, but that is not the case. That last walk was in bright and mild sunshine with just a gentle breeze blowing and hardly a cloud in the sky – I have the weather report for that day.

Women walking. Pumla Lolwana is not the only powerful and virtually nameless presence in my life. She has sisters. My notebooks record a few other destitute women who have walked across my path leaving their shadows on my work. In August of 1965 I made this entry about a lift I gave to an old African woman.

> We picked her up about ten miles outside Cradock. She was carrying all her worldly possessions in a bundle on her head and an old shopping bag. I'd guess about seventy years old. Cleft palate. A very hot day.
>
> Her story was that she had been chased off a farm after her husband's death about three days previously. She was walking to another farm where she had a friend. Later on she told us that she had nine children but didn't know where they were. She thought a few of them were in Port Elizabeth.
>
> After driving about fifteen miles it became obvious that she would never have reached her destination on foot that day. We asked her about this and she said she knew it and would have slept in one of the storm-water drains.
>
> She cried frequently. The first time was when I took the bundle (it was very heavy) off her head and put it in the boot and she realised she was going to get a lift. She told May she couldn't believe it. 'It was like a dream.' Then in the car, telling her story, she cried again, May comforted her. Finally, when we reached the gate where she wanted to get off and I gave her two of the three shillings left in my pocket, she cried again. I put the bundle on her head; May carried the shopping bag down an embankment to the gate and set her on her way. My last image of her is the thin, scrawny ankles between her old shoes and the edge of her old skirt, trudging away into the bush.

I suppose she stopped to cry a little and then went on, cried again later and went on, went on and on.

Barney – about her bundle: 'She still has a use for the things in her life.' And just her life; still using it – feeding it, sleeping it, washing it.

Her bundle consisted of one of those heavy three-legged iron pots, a blanket and an old zinc bath full of other odds and ends – all this tied together with a dirty piece of flaxen twine. In the old shopping bag I spotted a bottle of tomato sauce and Barney spotted a packet of Omo.

Finally only this to say: that in that cruel walk under the blazing sun, walking from all of her life that she didn't have on her head, facing the prospect of a bitter Karoo night in a drainpipe, in this walk there was no defeat – there was pain, and great suffering, but no defeat.

In 1968 this entry:

Another Coloured woman who might have been a model for my Lena. Lived somewhere in the bush along the Glendore Road. Worked for us for a short period about two years ago. Sense of appalling physical and spiritual destitution, of servility. Did the housework without a word or sound, without the slightest flicker of her 'self'. For some reason left us after about two months. Then some time later came back to see if we had any work. A stiflingly hot day . . . Berg wind blowing. In the course of the few words I had with her she seemed to be in an even more desperate condition that when we had last seen her – not so much physically, though that was still there, but poverty is poverty and at its worst there are no grades – it was a sense of her disorientation, almost derangement, of only a fraction of herself committed to and involved in the world around her. After telling the woman we had no work, she left us to try a few other houses. An hour or so later, the heat even more fierce by then, I left the house with snorkel and mask to do some skin-diving in the gulleys. I would not have moved out into that sun if it hadn't been for the prospect of the wet cool sea. I looked back at one point, just before going over the edge of the headland and down to the rocks, and saw the woman, empty-handed and obviously unsuccessful in her search for work, starting up the hill on her way back to Glendore.

That hill, the sun, the long walk. Possibly even a walk that Lena has not yet made . . . but will one day in the time that still lies ahead of her when she walks away with Boesman at the end of the play; a walk beyond the moment of rebellion – that possibility past, even forgotten – a walk beyond all the battles, the refusals, even tears. Surrender: defeat. A walk into the ignominy of silence, the world's silence and blindness, burdened now as never before by Lena's unanswerable little words. Why? How? Who?

And a few years later there was Patience – 'My English name is Patience' – with her baby on her back on the road outside Graaff Reinet.

I nearly didn't stop for her. She didn't signal that she wanted a lift or anything like that. Didn't even look up when I passed . . . I was watching her in the rear-view mirror. Maybe that's what told me there was a long walk ahead of her . . . the way she had her head down and just kept on walking. And then the baby on her back. It was hot out there, hot and dry and a lot of empty space. There wasn't a farmhouse in sight. She looked very small and unimportant in the middle of all that. Anyway, I stopped and reversed and offered her a lift. Not very graciously. I was in a hurry and wanted to get to the village before it got dark. She got in and after a few miles we started talking. Her English wasn't very good, but when I finally got around to understanding what she was trying to tell me it added up to another typical South African story. Her husband, a farm labourer, had died recently, and no sooner had they buried him when the *baas* told her to pack up and leave the farm. So there she was . . . on her way to the Cradock district, where she hoped to find a few distant relatives and a place to live. About my age. The baby couldn't have been more than a few months old. All she had with her was one of those plastic shopping bags they put your groceries in at supermarkets. I saw a pair of old slippers. She was barefoot.

So now it is Pumla walking. Was it purposeful? Heading straight to the tracks, her mind made up, very clear about what she was going to do? Holding the hands of her small children, crooning softly to the baby on her back, hoping the infant would stay asleep until the end? No. I reject that scenario. Lying there in the dark it surprises me to realise that even though all I know about Pumla Lolwana is her name and those of her children, I now have such a strong sense of her dark presence that I feel I have the authority to accept or reject possible scenarios concerning her. I see instead a random drift through that wasteland of lives called the Samora Machel Informal Settlement in search of something – a friend, or a relative, or the man, husband or boyfriend, who didn't come home with his pay packet the night before, a search for anything or anybody that could be a source of hope, a reason to live. She never found it and when she finally paused to rest, with little Sesanda asking 'Where are we going, Mommy? What's wrong, Mommy?', she was as the side of the railway tracks and a train was coming.

Women walking. Always women. Is the reason for that as simple as that early childhood memory I have of my mother, possibly the earliest? She was trudging heavily and wearily up the hill to where we lived and I had run to meet her. She was dispirited and depressed after a bad day in the bakery where she worked and it was a terrible shock to see her like that. She was the central and most important presence in my life. Seeing her defeated meant my whole world was in danger of collapsing. In the years that followed I saw my mother, metaphorically speaking, trudging up that hill many times. Her life was one long struggle for survival – for herself and her family. But she – and because of her, Lena and Milly and Hester and Miss Helen and all the other women in my work who draw their inspiration from my mother – was never defeated and that is the cardinal difference. Pumla Lolwana was. And it is that difference which maybe makes Pumla

Lolwana the dark mystery she will always be for me. There was no hope left.

Lying there in the dark I realise that the freight train has long since passed and all is silent once again, that soft sibilant silence of a sleeping suburban world. I can't even hear the surf, which is only a few hundred yards away from my bed.

8

29TH JUNE   I read:

> By Monday night nobody had claimed the bodies of the mother and her three children from the Salt River mortuary.

Nobody ever did. Pumla Lolwana's story ends in a sandy windblown cemetery on the Cape Flats where she and her children were given a pauper's burial. I realise suddenly that there is another personal connection here, this one going back all of fifty years to London where my wife Sheila and I are in Hampstead's Everyman Cinema watching *The Burmese Harp*. It is a beautiful film with its unforgettable central image of a Japanese Buddhist monk travelling through a war-ravaged Burmese landscape burying the bodies of fellow countrymen killed in battle and left to rot. At the time I didn't appreciate how profound an impression this film had made on me. I certainly recognised it as a deeply religious work of art but that is as far as it went. Now I see it as possibly the genesis of a theme – burying the dead – which has been there in my work from fairly early on and very much so in recent years. The story of Antigone captured my imagination at an early age. It is hard to think of a story that could have been more urgently needed in the Apartheid South Africa in which I grew up than that of the young girl defying the laws of the state because the

xli

unwritten laws of her conscience demanded that she bury her brother. It was inevitable that sooner or later Serpent Players – the black drama group I started in Port Elizabeth – would take on Sophocles' magnificent play. The story of that one lone voice raised in protest against what she considered an unjust law struck to the heart of every member of the group. This production had long term consequences, leading to the arrest of a member of the group who then staged a two-character version of the play – just Creon and Antigone – on Robben Island which in turn led eventually to the writing of *The Island*.

Some years later a photograph of two South African soldiers dumping the bodies of dead Swapo fighters in a mass grave in South West Africa led to the writing of *Playland*. A few years after that a newspaper item about unclaimed bodies in a police mortuary in the then Transvaal – victims of a black-on-black political massacre – resulted in the story of Lukas Jantjies, a Coloured man just a few years older than myself who is haunted by the thought of those unclaimed bodies. And now those of Pumla Lolwana and her three children in the Salt River mortuary. Is that what hooked me when I first read the story? Was that possibly the reason why I couldn't pass it over, consign it to oblivion as in fact time is trying to do to it? Is that why she has haunted me? Must I claim her? Yes, I want to do that. As I sit at my table this morning the deepest impulse in my heart is to claim them as mine. And why not! Nobody else wanted them. Maybe that is what I've been trying to do these past weeks at this table, claim her and her children and bury them in the blank pages of this notebook. With that thought I feel something has changed inside me in much the same way as the haunting stopped for Lukas Jantjies when he realised he had to bury the dead.

Every Sunday night here in Southern California I drive inland for two hours to Metta – a Thai Buddhist Forest

Monastery in an isolated valley – to join the Abbot and his five monks for the evening chanting and meditation. I centre my very simple Buddhist practice around one section of the chanting:

All human beings are the owners of their actions, heir to their actions, born of their actions, related through their actions and live dependent on their actions.

Whatever they do, for good or for evil, to that will they fall heir.

On my last visit I told the Abbot about Pumla Lolwana and her children and asked him if there was a prayer I could say or something I could do for the four of them. He suggested that I should dedicate whatever merit I earned from my next meditation to them. How do I do that, I asked? Say it, he said. Simply say aloud or to yourself 'I dedicate whatever merit . . .'

I started by saying their names aloud, because apart from a few impersonal facts, that is all I have of them:

Pumla Lolwana	35 years old
Sesanda Lolwana	5 years old
Andile Lolwana	3 years old
Lindani Lolwana	2 years old

Those four names have become infinitely precious to me. For all I know, here, ten thousand miles away from where they died, I might be the only person still thinking and saying them. They tell their own story – starting with those of the two boys, a simple story that speaks of a family that had grown stronger with each of their births; then came little Lindani, the daughter the mother had prayed and waited for. And then of course the mother herself: Pumla . . . which in Xhosa means to rest, to sleep, to find peace.

I was wrong when I started out to think that I needed to 'understand' what happened that Friday afternoon on the tracks between Philippi and Nyanga. That isn't why Pumla Lolwana stopped my life. It wasn't either to witness — that thin newspaper report did all that could be done by those who weren't there, who didn't see it. I had to claim her, for myself. Now, having done that, I have a sense as powerful as the one that made me stop a few weeks ago, that I can now move on.

9

30TH JUNE   I ended the day with a sunset walk next to the tracks. It was a quiet one. No trains passed. In spite of a very dry season the statice are still putting on a show. Out at sea there were a few distant pools of silvery light when sunshine has broken through a bank of cloud and spilt on to the water. Also, a cool and very refreshing breeze. I looked at my wristwatch: eight p.m. here, four a.m. in Cape Town. When I got back to my table I went online to get Cape Town's weather forecast: it promised a cloudless, sunny day with light winds and a maximum temperature of 19° C. The people of the Samora Machel Squatter Camp were in for a beautiful, mild winter's day.

The Train Driver was first presented by Eric Abraham
and the Fugard Theatre, Cape Town, during the opening
season of the Fugard Theatre on 19 March 2010. The
cast was as follows:

Simon (Andile) Hanabe Owen Sejake
Roelf (Rudolf) Visagie Sean Taylor

Director Athol Fugard
Co-Director Ross Devenish
Designer Saul Radomsky
Lighting Designer Mannie Manim
Music Director Mandisi Dyantyis
Lullaby Queen Jacob
Men's Vocals Simphiwe Mayeki, Xolani Momo,
  Luthando Mthi, Sonwabo Ntshata, Lizo Tshaka

The Train Driver received its first British performance,
in a Fugard Theatre production presented by Hampstead
Theatre and Eric Abraham, at Hampstead Theatre,
London, on 4 November 2010. The cast was as follows:

Simon (Andile) Hanabe Owen Sejake
Roelf (Rudolf) Visagie Sean Taylor

Director Athol Fugard
Designer Saul Radomsky
Lighting Designer Mannie Manim
Sound John Leonard

Characters

Simon (Andile) Hanabe
an old African man, a gravedigger

Roelf (Rudolf) Visagie
a train driver in his late thirties

Setting

An Eastern Cape graveyard
outside Motherwell

The action of the play takes place
in February 2001

THE TRAIN DRIVER

PROLOGUE

Simon is bareheaded and we can see a lot of grey hair. He holds a little woollen cap in one hand as he talks directly to the audience.

Simon My name is Simon Hanabe, I am the one who puts the nameless ones in the grave. This is how it happened. When I first see the white man . . . he is walking among the *amangcwaba* where the ones with names is sleeping. It is the first time I see that white man. Sometimes he goes down on the ground and I think he is reading the names but then he stands up and walks some more . . . and looking, looking. All the time he is looking at the *ingcwaba*. So I say to myself: Simon, what is this man doing here among our sleeping people? Who is he looking for? Then he sees me watching him and he comes to me and starts talking, but that time I didn't know what he was saying – his words were all mixed up like he was drunk. So he gets very cross with me when I shake my head and tell him I don't know what he is saying. So he leaves me and walks around some more. Then I see he gets tired and I feel sorry for him so I go to him and tell him that there is no white people sleeping there where he is looking in Shukuma. Only black people. And he says no, he isn't looking for a white people. He is looking for a black one without a name. So I show him where they are sleeping, the ones without names. There are many *ingcwaba* here and he asks me do I know who they are and I tell him no, I know who they are because these are the ones without names. And I ask him who he is looking for and he tells me it is *unfazi* . . . a woman . . . a young

3

woman with a baby on her back. I ask him if the baby is also dead and he says yes the baby is also dead.

Segue into . . .

The graveyard of Shukuma, a squatter camp on the outskirts of Port Elizabeth.

It is a rocky, weed-choked stretch of veld.

The graves are simple mounds of soil packed down with stones. To one side are a few identifying the person buried with a simple name board or a wooden cross – all weather-beaten. Most of the space however is taken up by nameless graves. Most of these have a piece of discarded junk on them: a rusty motorcar hubcap, an empty plastic bottle, etc. The wind has blown away a lot of the soil from some of them, which as a result now rise only a few inches above the ground. On one side there is a straggling wire fence and on the other a typical squatter camp shack. It is an image of desolate finality.

Standing among the graves and looking around helplessly is an exhausted and distressed Roelf Visagie. It has obviously been a long and hot day – his shirt is unbuttoned and hanging out of his trousers and he is wiping a sweaty neck and chest with a handkerchief.

Watching him at a distance and leaning on a spade is Simon Hanabe.

The time is late afternoon. In the course of the scene the light fades into twilight.

Roelf (*to Simon*) Mr Mdoda the undertaker remembers her. About four weeks ago. He said he brought her to you to bury.

Simon (*now going up to Roelf*) Then she is here. Because this is where they are, the ones without names. When Mr Mdoda bring me the next one, I dig the hole here.

He indicates a specific spot for the next grave.
   Roelf looks around, shaking his head in mixture of
despair and disbelief.

Roelf Fucking hell! What a miserable bloody ending to
your life's story. I wouldn't even bury my dog like this,
man!

   Goes to one grave and picks up an old motorcar
   hubcap.

And all this rubbish on the graves? What the hell is the
idea? Hey? Get to heaven faster with a Jetta hubcap?
Look at them all. Who the hell puts all this junk on the
graves?

Simon Me.

Roelf You?

   He walks among the graves, looking at the various
   items Simon has placed on them.

You put these here?

Simon *Ewe.* There is no flowers in Shukuma.

Roelf I see! So that is what it's supposed to be . . . respect
for the dead! Then why not just a simple cross, man? All
you need is two little sticks like that one over there . . .
and a piece of string . . . and then tie them together.

   Crosses his two forefingers and holds them up for
   Simon to see.

Remember Jesus? You people are also supposed to believe
in God and Jesus isn't that so?

Simon (*shaking his head*) Is no good to make cross.
People they come and steal it to make fire to keep warm
and cook food.

Roelf So now there is also no sticks in Shukuma . . . only rubbish!

A helpless gesture as he slumps to the ground, resting his back against a fence post.

No . . . I give up. *S'trues* God . . . I've had it. This is it. Where the hell do I go from here? Ja! Hell! That is where she deserves to be. I mean . . . Jesus . . . I spent nearly the whole fucking day walking that Swartkops bush trying to find the *pondok* where she lived or somebody that knew her.

I walked that bush three times – one time with a black policeman from the Motherwell Police Station and two times by myself. From one miserable bloody *pondok* to another. And every time I asked them: 'Is anybody here missing a woman and a baby?' Sometimes they would ask: 'What did she look like?' and I would tell them: 'She was a young woman with a red *doek* on her head, and a old grey blanket that was holding a baby on her back.' I know that description off by heart because that is what I saw. Then of course they would just shake their heads and sometimes I could see they wasn't even listening to me. A couple of times they hated me very much and then it was '*Suga wena*' or '*Voetsek witman*', which was okay because I wanted to say, 'And you fuck off as well' . . . and what's more I did. One guy was drunk and asked me if I wanted to fuck a black woman and said he would get me one. It's pathetic, man! Those people live like animals. No toilets so their places was always stinking of shit – if you will excuse the language – the children crawling around in the dirt with no clothes on. I told one women to wipe her baby's nose because he was eating his own snot. What made it worse is that I got so *deurmekaar* on those footpaths I would end up at the same *pondok* two or three times and start asking my questions until they would say, 'Why is the Baas asking us again?' It was too much for me, man. So then it's back to the police station, who send me to the morgue, and then the old chap there says it's Mr Mdoda, the undertaker, I must speak to because he always buries the ones without names, and finally Mr Mdoda sends me here. Here! Look at it.

He looks around, then gets up and makes one more limp attempt to find the grave of the woman he is looking for.

And you sure you don't know anyone who is buried here?

Simon I tell you, whiteman: this is the place for the ones without names.

Roelf What about this one. A man or woman? You know . . . *amadoda* . . . *abafazi*.

Simon (*shocked*) What you ask, whiteman! I don't open the bag and look. I dig and put them in. It is hard work now. I must dig deep because the dogs come. When I first come here to Shukuma there was no dogs in the bush. Now there is many and they are hungry. They come at night and try to dig them up.

He picks up a stone on one of the graves.

I put stones now on the graves to throw at them.

He moves slowly among the graves shovelling a little sand back on to the ones that are on the point of disappearing.

And then there is also the wind. When it is strong it blows the sand away. Too much wind! Sometimes it blows one days, two days, three days, four days, and Simon must sit there in his shack all the time and wait. I can't dig because the sand is getting in my eyes.

So why you want this woman with the red *doek*? Did she work for you in the house?

7

Roelf No.

Slumps down on the ground with his back to the fence post.

Simon Did she do the washing in the backyard?

Roelf No.

Simon Did she steal from you?

Roelf NO!

Simon Then when you find her *ingcwaba* what you do? You want to dig her up?

Roelf (*now extremely exasperated by Simon's persistent questions*) I want to find her because . . . Okay . . . you want to know why? Then I'll tell you . . .

He can no longer restrain himself from telling the truth.

Right now, my good friend . . . the way I feel right now is that if you can show me her grave I will stand there, take a nice deep breath and then I will swear at her until I am blue in the fucking face!

Simon (*shocked*) Curse her?

Roelf *Ja.* I want to swear at her until she knows she's a piece of black shit.

Simon *Dead* . . . no name . . . and you want to swear at her?

Roelf (*with vicious deliberation*) *Ja.* Give me her name . . . or show me her grave . . . and I will do it. *S'trues* God. In both official languages because I am fully bilingual. And don't think I am just talking about 'Go to hell,' and 'Your mother's cunt,' because I can do a hell of a lot better than that. I'll do it so that her ghost will hear me. I'll tell her how she has fucked up my life . . . the selfish

8

black bitch . . . that I am sitting here with my arse in the dirt because thanks to her I am losing everything . . . my home, my family, my job . . . my bloody mind! *Ja!* Another fucking day like this one and I won't know who I am any more or what the fuck I am doing! Jesus! Jesus! Jesus! Help me!

Roelf cannot contain the emotion that has been building up in him. Now at last it is released in stifled tears and sobs that shake his body. Simon is very disturbed by the other man's behaviour and presence. He tries to return to his attempts at tidying up the graves while at the same time looking around nervously and registering the onset of twilight.

Simon (*after a long pause*) Whiteman! You can't sit here. Just now it is getting dark and then this place is dangerous. If the *amagintsa* find you they will take out their knives. You don't belong here. You must go.

Roelf *Ama*-who?

Simon *Amagintsa.* The gangs . . . the young boys. The *tsotsis.* They won't like you.

Roelf (*sarcastically*) Like you do, hey! So what you waiting for? Go call them.

Simon Be careful. Don't make jokes, whiteman. You must go.

Roelf Go where? There's nowhere to go from here. This is it. All passengers off, please! End of the fucking line.

Pointing to the graves.

Look at them, for God's sake.

Simon They are sleeping now . . . and *wena*, you are awake. Go to your home!

Roelf Home? Don't you understand anything? I've crashed!

9

I was on the rails, I was going forward, everything up to schedule . . . until it all crashed. *Thanks to that woman with the red doek I don't know if I've got a home any more. I don't know if I've got a family any more, or a job or . . . ja . . . a life.* You said it: This is the place for the ones without names . . . and I think I'm one of them now. Roelf Visagie? Who the hell is he? You got your spade, so dig another grave, man.

> *Simon makes one more useless attempt to tidy the graves, but he is now even more disturbed by the other man's presence. He looks around apprehensively again before finally going up to Roelf.*

Simon When the *amagintsa* is finished with you they will come and do me. *Ja!* That is how it is with them. I am too old to run away. They will catch me. 'Why you let this white man sit here in our world, Simon? Why you let him come and sit here where our people is sleeping?' . . . And then they take out their knives again. (*Very firmly.*) Is not good! You come with me now.

> *Roelf doesn't move. After looking around again Simon prods him with his spade and speaks firmly.*

Hey! I say come with me! Wake up, whiteman. *Kom man!*

> *Roelf gets slowly to his feet and follows Simon.*

SCENE TWO

Simon's shack.
  The two men. Simon lights a candle.

Simon (*pointing to a corner*) You sit there tonight. Tomorrow you go somewhere else.

> *Roelf sits down in the corner indicated.*
>   *Simon goes to what is obviously his bed – a jumble*

*of old blankets on the opposite side – and settles
down, resting his back against the wall of the shack.
He studies Roelf.
The candle is on a wooden box next to his bed.*

Roelf (*looking around*) So this is your place . . . your
ikhaya . . . your home.

Simon *Ewe.*

Roelf *Ja,* well . . . as they say: no place like it, hey?
That's for fucking sure.

He shakes his head in disbelief.

If Lorraine – my wife – could see me now! She'd make
me soak in Clorox for a week before she let me get into
bed with her. God alone knows what she'd do with you,
my friend. Because she's very fussy, you know . . . specially
about bad smells and things like that. Hygiene! That's her
hobby. Give her a can of Lysol to spray around . . . you
know . . .

*He demonstrates Lorraine spraying the air with an
aerosol.*

Ssssss . . . Sssss . . . and she's a happy woman. Between
me and you though I think she carries it a little bit too
far. Like this dead woman I'm looking for . . .

Simon Red *Doek.*

Roelf That's the one. Well, you see, after the accident
I was thinking about her one night . . . well, to tell you
the truth I was thinking about her every bloody night . . .
you know how it is, man, when you switch off the light
and you lie there in the dark and your brain just won't
stop thinking . . . So I'm lying there in the bed in the dark
waiting for the pills to put me to sleep . . . and I was
talking to myself, but softly because I didn't want to wake
up Lorraine . . . so I was talking to myself about all that

happened and how it happened and about Red *Doek* because it just doesn't make sense you see, when the next thing I know is that Lorraine is sitting up in bed and shouting, 'Will you please shut up about that bitch! This house already stinks from her! I can smell her everywhere!'

How do you like that, hey? She's never seen her but now she can suddenly smell her everywhere. *Ja*, home sweet home. I know all about it.

Simon So why you want to swear at this woman with the red *doek*? What she do to you?

Roelf I don't know any more. I don't know if she did it to me or if I did it to her. All I know is she is dead and I am well and truly fucked-up.

Simon What you do to her?

Roelf That's a nice simple question. I think I killed her!

Simon Yo!

Roelf Yep. Simple as that. Everybody of course says I didn't . . . the other drivers, the Systems Manager sitting behind his desk, my wife . . . *Ja!* You want to hear Lorraine on that one!

(*Imitating his wife's voice.*) 'She was drunk, Roofie darling. Booze and pot. It's the same story with all of them.'

Thank you very much, Lorrie darling, but I know how I feel inside. It was me she was looking at when she went down. It is her face that haunts me every bloody night in my dreams!

Simon How you kill her?

Roelf Can you read?

Takes a very tired newspaper clipping out of a pocket and offers it to Simon.

12

Simon (*shaking his head and waving away the offered clipping*) No read.

Roelf I know . . . it was a stupid bloody question.

Opens the clipping and reads.

'December 12, 2000.'

'Mother and child die on railway tracks.'

Interrupting his reading.

Last Christmas! You get it? Christmas time? Funny hats and firecrackers and Father Christmas with a big cotton-wool beard, everybody Happy Happy Happy!

Simon Christmas box!

Roelf *Ja*, Christmas box. Everybody happy. The big piss-up!

He resumes reading.

'An unidentified woman with a child on her back stood on the tracks in front of an oncoming train and she and the baby were pulverised under the train's wheels. The seriously traumatised train driver looked on helplessly as . . .'

He interrupts his reading.

That's me . . . the 'seriously traumatised train driver' is me . . . Roelf Visagie. Do you know what traumatised means? Of course not. It means: fucked-up! Here . . . (*Tapping his head.*) Seriously fucked-up in here, my friend! And did you also hear 'looked on helplessly'? You at least know what that means, don't you? That means that the seriously traumatised train driver, who is me, could do fuck-all about it.

That's what they all jump on . . . Lorraine, Dennie my fishing buddie, Miss Conradie that little *poppie* with

13

her university diploma hanging on the wall giving me counselling sessions . . .

'You didn't do it, Mr Visagie. You couldn't stop the train in time. Isn't that so?'

'Yes, Miss Conradie, that is quite right – those big diesel jobs need fifty metres to stop. She stepped out on to the tracks when there was only about fifteen metres between us.'

'There, you see. And you couldn't swerve, could you?'

'That's also right, Miss Conradie. You can't swerve. But you see, Miss Conradie, I already know all that. So then if it wasn't me, then who was it? God? That's right. Because there was only God and me seeing how it happened. We were the only other ones who saw the look in her eyes, saw the baby's head peeping over her shoulder! So if it wasn't me, then was it HIM? God Almighty, who was stupid enough to make this bloody world in seven days. Yes, Miss Conradie. Stupid. Because I certainly wouldn't. But as it so happens, Miss Conradie, God was only a witness because it was Roelf Visagie who was tramping down so hard on the brake that the wheels was screeching on the tracks. It was Roelf Visagie not God there in the cab screaming to her to get out of the fucking way. And it was dear old Roelf again sitting on the side of the tracks vomiting when he saw how his train had "pulverised" her and her baby. And finally, Miss Conradie, let me ask you if you think God is also having nightmares every night when he looks into those big eyes with no hope in them.'

Yep, Simon. That is what I saw. Eyes that look as hopeless as those graves out there. Eyes that were ready for one of those graves out there.

Pause. It takes Roelf a good few seconds to recover from his emotional outburst.

14

Simon waits patiently, staring at him all the time.
Roelf goes back to the clipping and reads again.

'By Monday night nobody had claimed the bodies from the Mount Road mortuary. In the meantime the train driver is receiving counselling.'

There you have it.

Pause. He carefully folds the cutting and puts it away,
shaking his head in disbelief as memories flood back.

But you know what is interesting, Simon . . . If you were just watching me from the outside during those first few weeks after it happened you would have said what they all was saying, that Roelf Visagie is getting better. He's getting over it . . . he is on the mend. I tried to keep my mind off things by working in the garden, doing Christmas shopping with Lorraine – that is when we bought the Christmas tree – and just anything else you know that would keep my hands busy. I'm one of those guys that if his hands is busy, he's happy. The one thing that should have warned me that things were cooking up inside me, was the nightmares. Even with the pills that the doctor gave me I would still wake up with the fear of hell in my heart, man, because I was in the cab and she was there on the railway line waiting for me. It was getting so hard on Lorraine, because she had to be at work at the supermarket the next day, that I started sleeping on the pull-out sofa in the lounge. It is easy to see now that that was a big mistake because that meant I was right in there with the Christmas tree. Breaks my heart, man, when I think about it now. Because we were really all so happy when I put up the tree, and the children decorated it and I switched on the fairy lights. Lorraine and I had tears in our eyes as we played 'Silent Night, Holy Night' on the hi-fi. It didn't happen that night. It was a few nights later. Same old story. I took the sleeping pill, I fell asleep and then there she was again in front of me and this time there was also crowds of people on the side of the line watching it happen and cheering like it was some sort of sport going on. I was shit scared in the dream and I was shit scared when I was lying there with my eyes wide open because I sort of knew, lying there on the sofa, that she wasn't ever going to go away. So it was once again a case of 'Do something, Roelfie, just get up and do something.' There was a second box of fairy lights that I hadn't used so I decided to put them on the tree as well. I did that and then switched them all on and sat on the sofa looking at them blinking on and off and on and off. If you were sitting there with me now like we are sitting now in this *pondok* you would have seen me shaking my head because that is what I was doing, staring at those lights blinking on and off. It was like a fucking bomb ticking away inside me . . . the lights . . . On and off, on and off . . . and then suddenly 'the bomb' is exploding inside me, man. I think I must have looked like a wild animal that escapes from its cage and just wants to kill anything in front of it, anything it sees. And for me it was that stupid bloody Christmas tree blinking on and off and on and off. So I smashed it. *Finish and klaar*. I ripped the lights out of the wall like they was its roots and I picked up the tree and started smashing it on the floor and when I was finished there they were standing in the doorway, looking at me with frightened eyes. Lorraine and the kids. She was holding on to them as if I was going to smash them on the floor as well. All I could think of to say was, 'What the fucking hell are you all staring at?' And Lorraine said, 'These are your children, Roelf Visagie – go swear at your woman from the bush.' Then she took the kids into the bedroom and I could hear her lock the door. I heard her say to them, *'Jou pa is mal'* – 'Your father's gone mad.' But there you have it. 'Go swear at your woman from the bush.' One day I must tell Lorraine what a big favour she did me when she said that. When I heard those words it was like something just opened up inside me because I suddenly realised, you see, that that is what I wanted to do! *Ja!* I wanted to take a deep breath and then load up my lungs with every dirty thing I had ever heard and then say them into the face of that woman, who still stands there waiting for me in my dreams. I wanted those to be the last words she hears when my train hits her. Can you understand that? Look at what she did to my life, for God's sakes. If she wanted so much to kill herself why didn't she just take her baby and jump into the river. That would have done it. Why did she have to drag someone else – *me!* – into her shit? But the trouble was I didn't know her name!

I mean, you know how it is. When you talk to somebody in your mind you think their name, don't you? You don't just say 'Hey you this' and 'Hey you that'. You say their name and then you see them. And that is how the ball started rolling. There in the lounge, with Lorraine and the kids hiding away from me in the bedroom, standing there with the pieces of the Christmas tree lying around me, I suddenly had this wonderful feeling that if I could get her name and swear at her properly, just once, curse and swear her out in English and in Afrikaans, because I really am fully bilingual, everything would once again be all right. I know that sounds stupid now, but I'm telling you the truth, man. I just wanted to swear at her properly. That is how it all started which ends up with me sitting here with you.

Pause. A dry little laugh.

But, you see, the trouble was nobody could tell me her name! Nobody. Not Head Office, who had the official report of the accident, not the police who spoke to witnesses . . . nobody could tell me who she was! But then it was that Sergeant Boesak there in the Swartkops

17

police station listened to me and seemed to understand what I was going through. He was a good somebody – one of the old-fashioned sort of policemen, you know. It was him who said to me to go the mortuary and see if anybody has identified her dead body, because that is where she is lying. Well, to cut a long story short she wasn't there any more because they had handed the body over to Mr Mdoda for burial. He had the contract for burying the bodies that nobody wanted. Then Mr Mdoda sends me to you and now here we sit. Do you understand now, Simon? If I can stand beside her grave it would maybe be even better than just knowing her name. That's why me and you is going to go out there tomorrow and you are going to help me find it. You understand, Simon? One of those graves is hers and we are going to find it tomorrow. And stop shaking your head and looking so scared shitless. I am not going to dig her up, for Christ's sake. I just want to curse at her.

The two men stare at each other. Eventually . . .

Simon I sleep now.

He blows out the candle.
After a few seconds of silence the scene fades out to the sound of dogs barking and yelping in the background and Simon's snoring.

SCENE THREE

The graveyard.
Simon and Roelf stand in the middle of the graves.
It is obviously another hot day – Roelf is in his shirt sleeves, his jacket is hanging on one of the fence posts. He is making a supreme effort to control his impatience and frustration with Simon.

18

Roelf Think, Simon! Maybe four weeks ago Mr Mdoda comes to you with one big body and one baby body and he say to you put them in the same hole . . .

Holding up his forefinger.

Two . . . ?

Simon (*holding up his forefinger*) *Ewe . . . zimbini . . . is twee*!

Roelf Yes . . . *twee*! Mr Mdoda brings them to you . . . where did you bury . . . Where did you dig the hole with your spade?

No! No! Don't shake your head again. Any more head shaking, my friend, and the bloody thing will fall off your shoulders. Just think! Four weeks . . . one big body . . . one small body . . . one hole . . . where?

Simon looks around and then walks among the graves muttering 'Zimbini zimbini zimbini.' He is followed by a hopeful Roelf who in turn is muttering 'One big one, one small one, one hole.' Simon eventually pauses and looks down at a grave. An excited and suddenly apprehensive Roelf backs away.

Roelf This one?

Simon I think . . .

For a moment it looks as if he might be on the point of saying 'yes' but in the end he shakes his head.

No . . . not this one.

Roelf (*increasingly desperate*) No! Don't stop. Look some more. What about these over here?

Simon follows Roelf.

This one, hey? Or this one? Look at this one, Simon. It looks like it's quite a new one.

Simon (*finally nodding his head*) *Ewe . . . ewe . . .* is just so.

Roelf (*staring down at the grave in disbelief*) Jesus! This is hers? This is where you . . . *dis twee?*

Simon *Ewe, ja, dis twee . . .* this is where the dogs come last week and try to dig. So I must fill it up again. Two times! But it's a old, old one, not a new one. But the dogs dig deep and so when I fill it up it is looking like new one.

Roelf is now very angry and on the point of violence. A frightened Simon backs away from him. It is a dangerous moment.

Roelf What the fuck is going on with you, old man? Are you playing around with me? Do you think this is some sort of fucking game? Because if that's what you think it is, then you are playing with fire, old man. If you don't find her grave for me without any more farting around I'll take your bloody spade and dig up every one of them until I do find her . . . and then I'll dig a nice deep hole for you, and I bloody well mean it!

He leaves Simon and wanders among the graves.

Christ Almighty, just look at them. Look! Open your bloody eyes, old man, and look at them. This place is a bloody disgrace to humanity!

He stops at one of the graves, which has got a rusty motorcar silencer on it.

Have you got no respect for the dead? Because if that is the case then you are worse than those dogs in the bush. And you know why? Because these are human beings lying here and you are also supposed to be one as well.

He picks up the silencer and throws it away. In its place he picks up one of the stones from the grave.

If you got to mark them, use these, for God's sake. They not flowers but God did at least make them as well. And what's more . . . *Ja!*

An excited little laugh as an idea occurs to him.

Ja! You can even make a cross with them! Yes! Look . . .

He is on his hands and knees, placing stones on the graves.

See how easy it is. Long one down for his legs and then a short one across for his arms. Come on, Simon. Look! Doesn't that look better?

Simon is watching Roelf's deranged behaviour with disbelief and fear.
 Roelf moves to another grave where he makes another cross. His behaviour is becoming increasingly absurd.

Don't just stand there . . . roll up your sleeves and help me. You fetch more stones and I'll make the cross . . . I know how to do it, you see. You might make the cross upside down and I think that's they way they do it in devil worship. You'd be sending the poor bugger in the grave to hell instead of heaven. *Ja.* That's the way it works, you see. You should see my mother's grave. Lorraine and I took the children there a few days before Christmas to pray for her and wish her a happy Christmas in heaven. And flowers. A big bunch of . . . beautiful flowers . . .

Simon approaches Roelf warily.

Simon Stop now, whiteman . . .

Roelf has moved to another grave.

Whiteman! . . . Stop now . . .

Roelf Stop what?

Simon Stop what you doing.

Roelf What I'm doing is respecting the dead. You are the one who must stop putting junk on their graves.

Simon is now beginning to sense Roelf's inner distress. He speaks firmly but gently.

Simon You must stop now looking for her.

Roelf For who?

Simon For Red *Doek*.

Roelf Red *Doek* . . . ?

For a few seconds the name means nothing to him. When he realises who Simon is talking about, his hands, filled with stones, fall limply to his side.

That's right . . . Red *Doek* . . . I'm looking for her . . .

He is speaking very quietly.

. . . and her baby . . . You realise, don't you, Simon, that it was a woman . . . a mother . . . with her baby on her back that stepped out on to the rails . . . there in front of me . . . and waited . . . for me . . . for the end . . . staring . . . and waiting . . .

Pause. He looks at the stones in his hands and slowly makes one more cross on the grave in front of him. He then crawls away and sits again with his back up against a fence post. He speaks quietly.

My head is all fucked-up, isn't it? Totally *deurmekaar* now. My ma was like that before she died. Didn't even recognise me any more. Called me 'Ferdie'. Where the hell did that come from? There's no fucking 'Ferdie' in our family.

Pause.

You see, Simon . . . the trouble is I keep seeing Red *Doek*'s big brown eyes . . . flat nose . . . just like yours . . . her mouth closed tight . . . I keep seeing that in my head all the time like it was . . . you know . . . when she stood there.

Pause.

But she doesn't look like that now, does she? I mean . . . things happen to you down there in the ground . . . not so? It's not like the deep freeze we got at home – put in the nice fish you caught in the river and take it out six weeks later and there it is . . . good as new . . . thaw it out, salt and pepper and a big piece of butter in the frying pan . . . and there you have it. Fresh fried fish. But down there . . . things happen, hey. Worms and all that. Like what happened to poor old Arnie Vosloo in the *Mummy* pictures where he is the King of Egypt and climbs out of his grave – bits of flesh hanging on the bones, worms crawling around in his eyeballs. Jesus! Makes you think, doesn't it? All of them . . . some mother's children . . . one day you and me also . . .

Gesture to the graves.

And that's how it ends for everybody. Yes . . . make no mistake, my friend . . . black man or white man . . . the worms don't care about that . . . its all the same to them . . .

Another twilight is settling in.
A few yelps and howls from dogs in the bush.
Both men look in their direction.

Simon I think the dogs come tonight.

Roelf And they don't give a shit either, do they, about white or black? And you know what we call them, white men – the dogs? Man's best friend! How's that for a joke!

23

Mirthless little laugh.

That's a good one, hey? We got one of those little ones with curly white hair. Lorraine calls it Baby. I don't like it. Growls at me all the time. Bloody sure he'd like to dig me up one day when I'm dead.

Simon When I was little *inkwebkwana* I had two dogs. One white one and one black one.

Roelf Like me and you, hey? One white and one black! What was their names?

Simon The white one I call him *iWandle* because he is white like the sea when it washes the rocks. The black one is *Indudumo* . . .

Roelf *Indudumo* . . .

Simon *Ja*, the big noise in the sky when the rain is coming.

Roelf Thunder.

Simon *Ja!* Thunder in the sky.

Roelf So where were you when you were a little boy . . . where was your home?

Simon My home was far away, by Hluleka and my name that time was Andile. Andile Hanabe. Simon is my whiteman's name.

Roelf And you were happy.

Simon *Ewe* . . . because I walk all the time with my dogs by the sea and I try to catch the fish.

Roelf With a fishing rod?

Simon (*shaking his head vigorously*) *Aikona!* Is iWandle and Indudumo who do it.

Roelf They catch the fish?

Simon *Ja.* They good dogs. They see him the fish. There in the big *gat* with the water in it.

Roelf The rock pool.

Simon They see the fish in the water. They see him and they start barking and barking and I look and I also see him. So then I jump in the water, they also jump in. We chase the fish in that *gat*, man. He go this way and that way but we chase him and then is iWandle who bite him and he jump and I catch him. *Ja!* I catch him when he jump.

Roelf With your hands?

Simon *Ja!* With my hands I catch him.

Roelf A big one?

Simon Yo! Is a big one. That one time is a big one and I make my mother and my little sister very happy.

Smiling as he smacks his lips.

Ja. We like fry fish.

Roelf Yes . . . specially with nice soft fried potatoes.

Neither of them moves as the twilight deepens into night.

Simon Come on, Roofie . . . is getting dark and dangerous. We must go sit inside now. Come.

SCENE FOUR

Simon's shack.
Simon is ladling out half a tin of baked beans on to an old enamel plate – the other half stays in the tin. That done he breaks half a loaf of white bread into two pieces.

He takes one of the pieces together with the tin and a spoon to Roelf, who is sitting quietly in his corner.

Simon then settles down with the plate and eats with relish.

Simon Roelfie, here's your beans.

It is like I tell you – the *amagintsa* is there by the shop and they stop me and speak: 'Where you get the money, old man?' I don't tell them you give it. I tell them I save it. But I see they don't believe me. So they grab me and say to me: 'Be careful, old man. We come to visit you one night.' So there it is. I think they hear about you, Roofie.

Roelf Let them come. I'm not scared of a bunch of *tsotsis*.

Simon Hey, Roofie! You don't know this world.

Roelf What don't I know about your world, Andile?

Simon *Amagintsa* is like the dogs in the bush, always smelling for new ones to dig up and eat. Just so with the *amagintsa*. They are smelling you out now, Roofie. Very soon they will find you and eat you with their knives. Dogs got long teeth, *amagintsa* got sharp knives. *Pasop, witman*!

Roelf watches Simon eat – his own tin of baked beans and bread is still untouched.

Roelf Simon, do you believe in ghosts? You know, *spooke*. Are there *spooke* out there? You know . . . from the dead people.

Simon *Spirits! Spooke!*

Roelf That's right . . . *spooke*. Are their *spooke* out there?

Simon *Ewe*. Plenty of *spooke* out there.

Roelf Do you see them, Simon?

Simon I hear them. At night. When the dogs are digging I hear them. They don't like the dogs. So I go out and throw stones. I throw very good because I always hear one of them cry in the dog *language* . . . Yeeeee!

He laughs.

And then I hear the *ghosts* again. It is like the wind, Roofie. It is very sad. The dogs wake them up and they are not happy.

Roelf Do you speak to them?

Simon I sing to them. I sing like my mother sing to me when I was a little boy and she carry me on her back.

Simon sings a Xhosa Lullaby: 'Thula Mama Thula'.

Imfene mam' imfene yamthabath' umntwana
Wasuke wakhala wathi iyo. (Repeat.)

Khawuthule mama thula, thula mama thula,
Thula mama thula, thula yithi tu. (Repeat.)

Yamthabath' umntwana yambeka egxeni
Wasuk wakhala wathi iyo. (Repeat.)

[Hush, Mother, don't cry.
The baboon took the baby.
The baby cried out 'iyo'.

Hush, Mother, don't cry.
Hush, Mother, hush!
The baboon put the baby over his shoulder.
The baby cried out 'iyo'.]

Roelf You think they hear you?

Simon *Ewe.* They go back to sleep . . . And all is quiet again.

Pause.

Roelf Tell me, Simon, when you bury one of them are you by yourself? When it is just you there, by the . . . what do you call it . . . the hole where you put them in . . . the grave?

Simon The *incgwaba*. Sometimes Mr Mdoda stay and watch me dig.

Roelf So what do you feel, Simon? You know . . . when you put them in the grave . . . what do you feel in your heart . . . inside you?

Simon I am happy. Because Mr Mdoda pay me.

Roelf I know that, but don't you feel a bit sorry for them? A little bit sad?

Simon No.

Roelf Then why do you put something on the grave? Every grave you put something on it.

Simon Because I mustn't dig there again. When Mr Mdoda first give me the job I sometimes dig and then I see somebody is already sleeping there. So now I put something on top to tell me: 'No, Simon, someone is already sleeping here.' Why you ask me so much?

Roelf Why? Because . . . because it's one of your own people, for God's sake. It was certainly somebody's . . . I don't know . . . husband, or brother if it was a man or somebody's mother or sister, or wife if it was a woman. One thing I know for sure is that if I had to dig a hole and put one of my people in it, I'd have some very strange feelings inside me . . . even if I didn't know their name or who they were or what they were.

Pause. He is moving into unknown territory and is not sure of where he will end up.

But you know what's even more strange, Simon . . . ?

Simon What is even more strange?

Roelf (*it is not easy for him*) Out there this afternoon . . . there in the graves . . . when I got so difficult with you because you couldn't show me where Red *Doek* was buried . . . I got so cross with you because I was . . . Because . . . *Ja!* Because I was having strange feelings for all those poor buggers lying there and turning into mummies. Can you believe that?

A little snort of disbelief.

Ja! And because it was like that . . . the next thing I know is . . . You are not going to believe this, but I swear to God it's true . . . The next thing I know is that I didn't want to swear at her any more! Can you also believe that? It's true, man! I didn't want to swear at her because . . . I was thinking . . . I was thinking about those *pondoks* in the bush, about the smell of shit, about the man who asked me if I wanted to fuck a black woman . . . and I was thinking . . . she lived in one of those *pondoks* . . . she lived like that . . . *Ja!* That was what Red *Doek* called home. A young woman, a mother, with her baby! You get it? That is fucking hopeless, man. Think about it. Wouldn't you also want to go stand on a railway line and wait for the next train if that is all life has to offer you and your baby? And then to make it worse . . . she ends up here . . . in one of your *ingiwabas* or whatever you call them. And why? . . . Because that is still not the end . . . Because the big happy ending is that Nobody Wants Her! . . . Except the dogs.

The press clipping comes out of his pocket.

Remember what it said? Nobody came to claim her! Nobody wants her! And when we start looking . . . even we can't find her.

He takes a few seconds to regain control of his emotions. He now speaks very simply.

But suppose we did, Simon? Suppose you remembered where you buried a woman with a little baby, and you take me to that grave. What do I do? You understand now? I don't want to swear at her any more. What do I do? Go buy flowers to put there in place of the rubbish you put on it? That will help her a hell of a lot, won't it? Or say a prayer? To Him?

Pointing up.

If I ever get around to talking to Him it won't be a '*Asseblief Heilige Genadige God*', 'Please Most Holy and Merciful God' prayer that comes out of my mouth. You can rest assured of that, my friend.

Simon And now you want to see her ghost?

Roelf I know. Maybe.

Simon And you want to speak to her ghost? Yo!

Roelf Why not, for God's sake? . . . If you can sing to them, why can't I speak if there is things I want to say to her . . . or ask her. Oh fuck it . . . I don't know. And neither do you, my friend. (*Defensively.*) So stop looking at me like you now also think I am crazy.

Simon (*shaking his head*) Eat your *boontjies*, Roofie.

Roelf (*pushing his tin in Simon's direction*) I'm not hungry. You can have them.

Simon takes the tin and wastes no time tucking into it.
Roelf sits back and stares into space.
The scene fades out on that image of the two men.

SCENE FIVE

Night.

In the dimly lit interior of the shack we see Roelf stand up, quietly leave the shack and walk among the graves.

Roelf Red *Doek*? I don't know your name, so that is what Simon and I call you. He is the man who buried you.

Pause.

Can you hear me? I want to talk to you . . . but . . . it's sort of stupid . . . I don't really know where you are. Are you lying here in the ground? Or are you up in heaven? Not hell. No ways. That's for sure. If all they say about God Almighty is true – that he loves all of us – then you are certainly not down there at the big barbecue. Miss Conradie told me not to worry so much because 'your soul is now at rest'. Like hell, hey! At rest? When your last memory of life is a white man staring at you from the cab of a diesel locomotive as you go down under its wheels. So what I am going to do, Red *Doek*, is imagine Simon is right and that your ghost comes out of the grave at night and walks around here at night . . . that I can talk to you like you was standing right here in front of me . . . listening to me.

Pause.

It's strange, you know. Sometimes I think I've got so much to say to you that this one night won't be long enough . . . but then at other times I think there is nothing to say . . . that for me you will for ever just be Red *Doek* standing there on the tracks, and that for you I will for ever just be a white man staring at you in the few seconds before you die. But that is not right, is it? It can't be as simple as that! I mean . . . look what has happened . . . to us . . . to me and you. You and your baby are dead . . . buried in one of these *ingiwabas,* and I am . . . I don't know what. I'm trying all the time to understand it all, but all I know is that you are dead and Roelf Visagie is fucked-up in his head like never before. So what it comes down to is that it is all about you and me, and that is what makes it so complicated for me. You see, I don't really know what your story is – who you are, where you come from, what's your name . . . that sort of thing. It's not so bad now as it was at the beginning when all I could say to myself was that my train . . . me! . . . Roelf Visagie . . . killed a black woman with a red *doek* and a baby on her back. But now, thanks to all I've seen and heard in the past few weeks, like that walk in the Swartkops bush looking for your *pondok,* thanks to all I've thought and what Simon has said to me and what this place looks like, I got some sort of idea, some sort of feeling about your world. You see, Red *Doek,* most of us white people got no idea about what it's like because our world is so different! We always think we know – like Lorraine, my wife – she thinks she knows everything about you people . . . and I did as well . . . but the truth is, we don't.

But now, like I said, I got some ideas . . . I got some good guesses going about your world and why you stood there on the railway line waiting for me and my train. One of my guesses is that I think it's all about hope. You know what I mean . . . Hope! . . . Hoping good things are going to happen to you, that tomorrow is going to be better than today. which was terrible. And there you have it.

Pause.

I don't know what it is like to live without hope, to give up.

Because you did, didn't you? That is why you did what you did because you didn't believe any more that good things was going to happen to you and your baby. I'm thinking about it all the time now, trying to imagine what it was like for you. It is very dark in Simon's shack when he blows out the candle so I lie there in that dark and I think to myself . . . was it like this for her? Was it dark like this for Red *Doek*? Darker . . . I say . . . because her darkness was somehow inside her and how the hell do you light a *stompie* candle there? When I think about that, when I try to imagine what that is like, I get frightened. Yes! Believe it or not, but I still get scared of the dark.

So then what now, you ask? I've got to do something! I know it's too late for you to do anything, but I still got a chance. What's more, Red *Doek*, it feels very urgent that I do something, because it feels like I am losing you and if that happens, if I can't even remember your face any more, then I really will go mad like they all say I am. But I am not, and to prove it I know what I must do now. I've got a newspaper story here in my pocket which is all about me and you . . . There is one thing that always sort of upsets me in a special way when I read it . . . it's where it says that 'nobody claimed her'. Did you know that? Did you know that when you and your baby was lying there in the Mount Road mortuary nobody came to claim you? A mother and her baby and nobody wanted them! Can you believe that? Because you know what the Bible says, don't you? We was all made in His image . . . you . . . me . . . Simon . . . every human being . . . made in His image. But now you are lying here in the place for the ones without names because nobody wanted you. Well, that is not the way it is any more because now I hold up my hand and say: 'I Claim Her' . . . me . . . Roelf Visagie . . . the driver of the train what killed her . . . wants her to be his. *Finish and klaar*. You are mine . . . and God is my witness tonight even as he was when it all happened. You see, Red *Doek*, if I did lose you . . . if I ever, for one day, forget what happened to me and you there between Perseverance and Dispatch, then God must send me off to hell when I die.

Simon comes out of the darkness.

SCENE SIX

The shack. Evening. The candle is lit.
Another meal. This time Simon is spooning out smooth apricot jam on to half a loaf of white bread, which he hands over to Roelf. He then settles down to eat the other half with scoops of jam out of the tin.
Roelf is quieter and seemingly at peace with himself.

Simon Roofie! There is bread and apricot jam. Come, Roofie, let's eat.
You like, Roofie? Apricot jam.

Roelf *Ja.* I like.

Simon *Ja . . . is lekker!* A little sweetness is good.

Roelf The best is golden syrup on fresh white bread when it is still nice and warm.
You ever had that?

Simon Never.

Roelf You must try it some time. Lyle's Golden Syrup. When I was a little boy and we didn't have jam or syrup my ma use to sprinkle white sugar on my bread.

Simon When I was young there by Hluleka, me and my father, used to look for wild honey in the bush, it's also nice.

Pause.
Roelf still hasn't touched his bread and jam.

Simon So what you thinking, Roofie?

Roelf Nothing.

Simon Then why you no eat? Why you say nothing?

Roelf Nothing more to say, Simon. So I was just thinking about going home. I can't stay here.

Simon Is good you go home. When you go?

Roelf I don't know.

Simon Maybe tomorrow is good.

Roelf Maybe.

Simon Why you not say yes, Roofie?

Roelf Because . . . I don't know . . . Because . . . *Ja!* . . . Because it doesn't feel like it is finished yet.

Simon What?

Roelf Simon . . . What this? Why that? I don't know every bloody thing!

Pause.

Being here doesn't feel finished.

Simon stares at him uncomprehendingly.

You understand, don't you?

Simon (*shaking his head*) No.

Roelf Well, don't let it give you sleepless nights, my friend, because to tell you the truth . . . neither do I. I want to go home to Lorraine, my kids, Prissie and Morné, even the fucking dog, Baby. But something is holding me back. We are never going to find her grave out there. I don't want to swear at her any more. Just the opposite, man. She's mine now, Simon, she is now mine . . . you understand? I don't want to swear at her any more because now she's mine. I claimed her.

35

Simon (*shocked*) What you saying? You want to marry her?

Roelf Oh for God's sake, Simon, give me a break!

Simon She's lying in the ground and you want to marry her?

Roelf No, man, you didn't understand me. It's not like that! It's more like . . . Let's just say I don't know what it means when I say she is mine, but I know she is, because I feel that way inside my heart and so I claimed her. Nobody else wanted her, Simon . . . I do, and that's the end of it.

And I will also tell you that I know when that happened . . . when she became mine like nothing else in my life has ever really been mine before . . . it was when we looked into each other's eyes in the few seconds before she and her baby died . . . underneath me. And you want to know something else, Simon? Maybe it was like that for her also. *Ja!* Have you thought about that? That I was the last human being she saw. There was no hatred in her eyes, you know, Simon, no anger . . . just me . . . she saw me.

  Pause.

If I had known then what I know now, if I had felt then what I feel now, then I would have asked them there in the mortuary to let me bury her. I mean it.

  Pause.

But I didn't . . . and maybe that is what it's all about . . . maybe that's why this doesn't feel like it is finished.

  Pause.
  Simon is staring silently at Roelf.

Come on, man. You of all people must know what I mean. You take your spade and then you dig a hole . . . you dig it nice and deep so that the dogs can't get at it . . . you put the body in . . . right? And then you put all the sand back on top of it . . . not so? No . . . I almost forgot . . . you put something on top of it so that you don't dig there again. But then it's over. Finished. You walk away. That's what I can't do, Simon. Walk away.

Simon, still eating bread and jam, is studying Roelf thoughtfully. After a few seconds he pushes his food aside, stands up slowly, goes to the doorway and looks out over the graves.

Simon Roofie . . .

Roelf *Ja?*

Simon How many is sleeping there?

Roelf I don't know. If you want me to, I'll count them all for you tomorrow.

Simon Tomorrow there is one more. Mr Mdoda see me there at the shop when I am buy the jam and he tell me he bring me another nameless one tomorrow.

Roelf Okay. I'll count them after you buried him.

Simon, shaking his head, turns and faces Roelf.

Simon No. Not me.

He fetches his spade and offers it to Roelf.

You must dig the hole.

Roelf Me? Why me?

Simon Because you must put her in.

Roelf It's a woman?

Simon I don't know. But we say it is a woman. We say it is Red *Doek*. So tomorrow you bury Red *Doek*.

Roelf What the hell is going on with you, Simon?

Simon Is just like you said, Roelfie. You dig . . . you dig deep hole . . . then you put her in . . . Then you cover her up. Then you go get stones and put them like you like it on top . . . and then, Roelfie . . . I think then it is finished for you . . . and you can walk away . . . you can go home.

Roelf takes the spade.

Roelf Okay.

Simon goes back to his corner, settles down and then blows out the candle.
After a few seconds of darkness . . .

Simon!

A few more seconds of silence and then we hear Simon's snoring.

Simon. I'll do it . . .

There is enough dim light in the shack for us to see Roelf stand up and quietly leave the shack. Still holding the spade he stands among the graves for a few seconds then goes to the spot which Simon had earlier indicated was for the next grave and starts digging.
Lights fade out completely on the image of Roelf digging.

EPILOGUE

Simon This is where we find him. Here in the ground. In this hole is where the *amagintsa* bury him after they kill him. Roofie himself was digging this hole when the *amagintsa* come. *Ewe!* One time in the night I wake up and I see Roofie is gone so I look outside and I see him here digging. I call him but he says he is digging the hole for the new one that Mr Mdoda is bringing and that I must go back and sleep. So I go back and sleep but then I wake up again and I hear the *amagintsa* come. I hear the shouting and swearing and then it is all quiet. When Mr Mdoda come in the morning with the new one, nameless one, for me to bury, we come here and we see there is blood, a lot of blood all around here. So Mr Mdoda ask me what happens here, so I tell him about Roofie. Mr Mdoda gets very cross and swears at me and then he goes and fetches the *polisie*. When they come they make me dig here and then we find Roofie. *Kaalgat*. No clothes. That's how the *amagintsa* leave him. The *polisie* grab me and say: 'Why you kill the whiteman with your spade?' But I say to them: 'No! It wasn't me!' So the policeman says that I lie and that I am drunk because 'there is blood on the spade'. But I say to them: 'No . . . I am not drunk. It is the *amagintsa* who kill him. They take out their knives and do it.' And then Mr Mdoda who is also standing there tells them: 'Yes, it is the *amagintsa* who did it.' So then the policeman say to me: 'Why you let this white man die here? Why you let him mess with our people?' So then I do what Mr Mdoda tell me to do: I tell them I don't know the white man. I never seen him before. Then they take him away and also my spade. And I say: 'No, you mustn't take my spade because I must bury the new one.' Then the black policeman tells me they must take the spade because there is blood on it. When they are gone Mr Mdoda tells me he is finished with me and that he will get somebody else to bury the new nameless one. So there it is. I haven't got a job and now also I haven't got a spade.

He stands there, his hands held out in a helpless gesture.

The End.

Glossary

All in Xhosa, unless indicated as Afrikaans.

abafazi   dead man
aikona   expression of dismay: 'No, you're wrong!', I disagree
    (*Afrikaans*)
amadoda   dead woman
amagintsa   hoods, hoodlums that go in gangs
amangcwaba   graves
Andiyasi. Ek weet nie   Man or woman, I don't know (*Afrikaans*)
Asseblief Heilige Genadige God   Please Almighty and Merciful
    God
baas   boss (*Afrikaans*)
baie snaaks   very strange (*Afrikaans*)
beneuked   annoyed (*Afrikaans*)
Bietjie soeterigheid is goed   A little sweet is good (*Afrikaans*)
braai   barbecue (*Afrikaans*)
daar is bloed op die graaf   there is blood on the spade (*Afrikaans*)
Daar is brood met appelkoos jam, jong   There is bread and fresh
    apricot jam (*Afrikaans*)
daar's jou boontjies   here's your beans (*Afrikaans*)
dagga   pot, marijuana
deurmekaar   confused, out of one's head (*Afrikaans*)
die donderweer dar bo   the thunder up above (*Afrikaans*)
dit word donker   It's getting dark (*Afrikaans*)
doek   headscarf (*Afrikaans*)
dog taal   the language of dogs (*Afrikaans*)
donderweer   thunder (*Afrikaans*)
dood   dead (*Afrikaans*)
Een groot lyf, een klein lyf, een gat . . . waar?   One big body, a
    little body, one hole . . . right? (*Afrikaans*)
Ek het haar geeis   I claimed her (*Afrikaans*)
Ek will haar uitskel   I want to curse her (*Afrikaans*)
en jy will haar uitskel   and you want to curse her (*Afrikaans*)
En met haar spook praat? Yo!   And speak with her ghost? Right?
    (*Afrikaans*)

En nou jy will haar spook sien?   And now you want to see her ghost? (*Afrikaans*)
ewe   yes (*Afrikaans*)
Ewe, ja, dis twee   Yes, that's it, two times (referring to a grave that's been dug up) (*Afrikaans*)
ewe zimbini is twee   look, (that's it), two bodies (*combined Afrikaans and Xhosa*)
finish and klaar   all over, that's it, to sum it up   (*Afrikaans*)
gevaarlik   dangerous (*Afrikaans*)
goeie honde, daar in die middel . . .   good dogs, there in the middle . . . (*Afrikaans*)
Hayi   Yes
hy word gesond   he's getting better, healing (*Afrikaans*)
ikhaya   home
indudumo   thunder
ingcwaba   grave, mispronounced as *ingiwaba* by Visagie
inkwebkwana   kid, boy
iWandle   white-cap of a wave
ja   yes (*Afrikaans*)
jou ma se moer   'your ma's a whore,' or 'fuck your mother' (*Afrikaans*) curse phrase
jou pa is mal   'your father's nuts, gone mad, out of his mind' (*Afrikaans*)
Jy will haar trou?   You want to marry her?
kaalgat   naked (*Afrikaans*)
kak   shit, trouble (*Afrikaans*)
klippies   stones (*Afrikaans*)
Kom, laat ons eet!   Come, let's eat (*Afrikaans*)
kom man   come on, man (*Afrikaans*)
kom man, dis gevaarlik hier buite   come on, it's dangerous to be out here (*Afrikaans*)
lekker   delicious (*Afrikaans*)
lekker slap chips   tasty French fries (*Afrikaans*)
lieg   lie (*Afrikaans*)
Moenie kak praat   You're talking nonsense (*Afrikaans*)
Nee man! Jy't my nie verstaan nie   No, you don't understand (*Afrikaans*)
Nee man, dis jy wat kak praat   No, you're talking nonsense
neuk with   mess with (*Afrikaans*)

no ukufunda   I can't read, 'no read'

ou   old (*Afrikaans*)

pasop, witman   Be careful, whiteman (*Afrikaans*)

poep bang   so nervous, like you've seen a ghost, shit scared
     (*Afrikaans*)

polisie   police (*Afrikaans*)

pondok   shack, made with whatever is available

poppie   'doll', 'darling little girl', disparaging way to address a
     woman (*Afrikaans*)

skel   curse, swear (*Afrikaans*)

spooke   ghosts (*Afrikaans*)

steenbras   delicious lagoon fish (*Afrikaans*)

stompie   stump, such as a short candle   (*Afrikaans*)

suga wena   fuck off

s'trues God   I swear by God (*Afrikaans*)

Sy lê in die grond en jy will met haar trou?   She's buried under-
     ground and you want to marry her? (*Afrikaans*)

tsotsi   hoodlums, often young gang boys

umshologo   ghosts

unfazi   woman

veld   open rural spaces grassy, or with low scrub and bushes,
     grazing areas (*Afrikaans*)

Verstaan jy? Ek will nie meer   Do you understand? I won't curse
     her (*Afrikaans*)

vloek   curse (*Afrikaans*)

vloek nie want sy is nou myne   Because she is now mine (*Afrikaans*)

voetsek, witman   fuck off, white man

vuka   wake up

wat is   what is (*Afrikaans*)

wena   go

*When I was inkwenkwe me and my tata, ons gaan daar by die bos,
     ons kry die wilde heuning. Is ook lekker*   When I was a little
     boy, my aunt and I went into the bush to get wild honey. It was
     very sweet (*Afrikaans*)